HOW TO GET THE
BEST DEAL FROM YOUR EMPLOYER

HOW TO GET THE BEST DEAL FROM YOUR EMPLOYER

A Practical Guide for Executives
Second Edition

MARTIN EDWARDS

KOGAN PAGE

First published in 1988 entitled *Executive Survival: A Guide to Your Legal Rights*
Second edition 1991

Apart from any fair dealing for the purposes of research or private study, or criticism or review, as permitted under the Copyright, Designs and Patents Act, 1988, this publication may only be reproduced, stored or transmitted, in any form or by any means, with the prior permission in writing of the publishers, or in the case of reprographic reproduction in accordance with the terms of licences issued by the Copyright Licensing Agency. Enquiries concerning reproduction outside those terms should be sent to the publishers at the undermentioned address:

Kogan Page Limited
120 Pentonville Road
London N1 9JN

© Martin Edwards 1988, 1991
Martin Edwards has asserted his right to be identified as
author of this work in accordance with the Copyright, Designs and
Patents Act 1988.

British Library Cataloguing in Publication Data
A CIP record for this book is available from the British Library.

ISBN 0-7494-0418-3
ISBN 0-7494-0258-X Pbk

Printed and bound in Great Britain by
Biddles Ltd, Guildford

Contents

Introduction	**11**
1. Taking Up a Job	**15**
1.1 Preliminaries 15	
1.2 The employer's freedom to recruit 17	
1.3 Are you an employee or self-employed? 18	
1.4 Directorships 20	
1.5 Accepting an offer 20	
1.6 Changing your mind 21	
1.7 Are you breaking an existing contract? 22	
1.8 Probationary periods 24	
1.9 Illegal agreements 24	
2. Your Employment Contract	**25**
2.1 The framework 25	
2.2 Letters of appointment 26	
2.3 Written particulars of employment 27	
2.4 Service agreements and back-up documents 30	
2.5 Implied terms 31	
3. Checking the Basics	**33**
3.1 The need to check 33	
3.2 Who are you working for? 34	
3.3 When does your job begin? 36	
3.4 Job title and duties 37	
3.5 Place of work 38	
4. Pay and Benefits	**40**
4.1 The money side 40	
4.2 'Golden' payments 41	

    4.3 Salary 42
    4.4 Commission 43
    4.5 Bonus 44
    4.6 Other payments 44
    4.7 Benefits 44

5. Restrictions on Your Freedom — 48
    5.1 What to watch for 48
    5.2 Documents and copyright 49
    5.3 Inventions and patents 50
    5.4 Trade secrets and confidential information 51
    5.5 Involvement in another business 52
    5.6 Garden leave 53
    5.7 Competition after you leave 55

6. When Will Your Job End? — 58
    6.1 Looking ahead 58
    6.2 Retirement 59
    6.3 Notice 59
    6.4 Fixed-term contracts 61

7. Working Overseas — 63
    7.1 Special problems 63
    7.2 Which legal system applies? 63
    7.3 Do you lose your statutory rights? 64
    7.4 Protecting your position 66
    7.5 Miscellaneous provisions 67

8. Coping with Change — 69
    8.1 The need for flexibility 69
    8.2 Keeping a job file 70
    8.3 Talking about problems 71
    8.4 Changes within the scope of your contract 72
    8.5 Refusing to change 73
    8.6 A change of employer 74

9. Personality Clashes and Discrimination — 76
    9.1 Conflicts at work 76
    9.2 Incompatible individuals 76
    9.3 Sexual harassment 78
    9.4 Sex and race discrimination 78

10.	**Criticisms of Your Job Performance**	**80**
	10.1 Is anything wrong? 80	
	10.2 Opportunities to improve 82	
	10.3 Special problems 83	
	10.4 Can you be sued? 85	
11.	**Sickness and Absence From Work**	**86**
	11.1 The risks 86	
	11.2 Special cases 87	
	11.3 Consultation and investigation 88	
	11.4 The decision 90	
	11.5 Persistent intermittent absenteeism 90	
	11.6 Maternity leave 91	
12.	**Disciplinary Complaints**	**92**
	12.1 The problem 92	
	12.2 Fair procedures 96	
13.	**Are You Redundant?**	**100**
	13.1 Job insecurity 100	
	13.2 What is redundancy? 101	
	13.3 When redundancy is in the air 103	
	13.4 Offers of alternative employment 106	
14.	**Redundancy Selection and Consultation**	**108**
	14.1 Why have you been selected? 108	
	14.2 The selection group 108	
	14.3 Selection factors 109	
	14.4 The consultation process 111	
	14.5 Trade union consultation 111	
	14.6 Individual consultation 112	
15.	**Constructive Dismissal**	**115**
	15.1 What does it mean? 115	
	15.2 Has the contract been broken? 116	
	15.3 How badly has your employer behaved? 118	
	15.4 How to respond 118	
	15.5 Practical implications 120	
16.	**The Threat of Dismissal**	**122**
	16.1 The need for awareness 122	
	16.2 Have you been dismissed? 123	

16.3 What is the date of dismissal? 126

17. Valuing Your Statutory Rights — 129
17.1 What is your job worth? 129
17.2 Redundancy payments 130
17.3 Unfair dismissal basic award 130
17.4 The compensatory award 131
17.5 Quantifying the compensatory award 132
17.6 Deductions 134

18. What is Your Contract Worth? — 136
18.1 Wrongful dismissal 136
18.2 Salary during the notice period 138
18.3 Motor car 139
18.4 Pension rights 140
18.5 Commission and bonuses 140
18.6 Other benefits 141
18.7 Hurt feelings 141
18.8 Deductions 142
18.9 Overlap with unfair dismissal 144

19. Termination Package Deals — 146
19.1 The gentle art of compromise 146
19.2 Negotiating techniques 147
19.3 Tax implications of termination payments 149
19.4 Other parts of the package 151
19.5 'Full and final settlement' 152

20. Going to Law — 155
20.1 The right approach 155
20.2 Arbitration 156
20.3 Avoiding dismissal 157
20.4 Are you eligible for rights? 157

21. Moving Elsewhere — 160
21.1 References 160
21.2 Written statement of reasons for dismissal 160
21.3 How free are you to move? 161
21.4 Aggressive recruiting 162
21.5 Taking stock 163

Appendices **165**
  1. Typical service agreement for a director or other senior executive 167
  2. Table of cases 176

Useful Addresses **178**
Further Reading from Kogan Page **179**
Index **181**

Author's note

This book is intended for any business executive who is not completely sure that he or she has a job for life. It seeks to highlight the legal issues which, in my experience, most often affect security of employment.

To survive in a competitive and sometimes ruthless world, it helps to understand how the law affects your position at work. But you need to know more than that: not just what to do when things go wrong, but how to anticipate problems and how best to avoid them. As J P Morgan once said, 'I don't hire a lawyer to tell me what I cannot do; I hire him to tell me how to do what I want to do.' In that spirit, the main focus here is on suggesting a positive approach.

Over the years, I have talked over this fascinating and important subject with many employers, employees and professional colleagues. In particular, for continuing help and encouragement of varying kinds, I would like to record my grateful thanks to my wife Helena and my partners at Mace & Jones.

Martin Edwards
Liverpool, 1991

Introduction

The race is not always to the swift, nor the battle to the strong – but that's the way to bet. Damon Runyon didn't have the problems of business executives in mind, but his words are worth taking to heart.

It is a fact of commercial life that few employees, however skilled, are indispensable for more than a short period of their careers – if at all. The victims of many a boardroom coup have learned that to their cost. To get the best deal from your employer at the start of, during and at the end of your employment, you need to be realistic.

You also have to appreciate that negotiating with your employer involves different considerations from bargaining with a customer or supplier. Plenty of books give advice on commercial negotiating techniques, but in the job context their words of wisdom must be applied with care.

When you are negotiating about your own job, it is hard to be detached. There is an old saying that a solicitor who acts for himself has a fool for a client. Equally, when discussing your own terms of employment, you may find it hard to judge objectively which points to press and which to concede. The danger is all the more acute if you lack a sophisticated and up-to-date knowledge of key areas of employment law.

Inept negotiations may cost you a new job which you had thought was in the bag. An even greater risk is that in handling severance negotiations you may either sell yourself short or, conversely, push your employers too far. The result can be disappointment or, worse, expensive litigation.

It is often helpful to seek advice from a professional with specialist experience of job-related negotiations. Some management consultants and accountants fit the bill, although they frequently lack the in-depth understanding of the technical but important issues of legal detail which underpin the terms of the contract or of the severance deal. Solicitors can offer the necessary degree of expertise – provided you consult someone with sufficient 'hands-on' experience of employment negotiations; the person who bought or sold your last house is unlikely to be suitable. Even if you do have the assistance of an outside adviser, you may prefer him or her to remain in the background – simply making the bullets for you to fire. Involving lawyers directly in job negotiations is, however unreasonably, looked on askance by many employers.

In practice, few executives ask for help when negotiating the terms of their employment contract; they are much more likely to seek advice only when facing dismissal. This is a pity, for the terms agreed when your job starts will have a crucial bearing on the strength or weakness of your position when the end of the road comes in sight.

The success or failure of employment negotiations cannot be judged in quite the same way as that of other business deals. The size of your remuneration package or golden handshake is obviously crucial. But there are other important matters which you need to check with care. For example, does your contract give you a decent measure of job security? For reasons explained later, if you can negotiate a lengthy notice period, that may justify your making many other concessions on the wording of the contract. You should also ascertain whether your future job mobility will be hampered if and when you leave the company. Your position may be governed by restrictive covenants covering two or three pages of closely typed legal jargon – which could have a major impact on your long-term career. You need to know what the gobbledegook means.

This book offers a practical guide through the legal maze. For convenience, most of the discussion that follows refers to employees of limited companies, but the same principles are often relevant to people employed in the public sector and those who work for trade associations and other organisations. Some of the specific problems faced by executives (or would-be executives) who are female, members of ethnic minorities or trade unionists are touched on briefly, but this book is not designed to provide a detailed account of discrimination law or collective labour rights. Those subjects are well covered in other texts. Employers and executives are generally referred to here in the masculine gender; this is simply for the sake of convenience.

The opinions expressed here should not be mistaken for categoric statements of legal principle. Employment law is beset by

Introduction 13

uncertainties. When, after all, is a dismissal 'unfair'? What is the length of the 'reasonable' notice of dismissal to which you are due? One can suggest realistic guidelines for matching the legal rules to the personal circumstances of individual readers, but there are few universal answers. 'Everything depends upon the circumstances' is the inescapable catch-phrase of industrial tribunals and the higher courts. Accepting that, most employees are likely to say: 'Fair enough, but how can I find out where I stand?'

Numerous past cases are discussed in this book: there is no better way of illustrating what can happen in practice. You can learn from the misfortunes of others, although you should not overestimate the importance of precedents. As Lord Justice Lawton said a few years ago, 'a surfeit of case law in employment law can have the same disastrous effect that a surfeit of lampreys had on King John'.

Even if this book were two or three times its present length, it could not do more than offer a selective guide to the vast array of legal rules affecting employment. The text deals with the law of England and Wales, although many points have equal force in Scotland and Northern Ireland. The most important statute, the Employment Protection (Consolidation) Act 1978, is referred to simply as the Consolidation Act.

No book with a legal slant which is designed as a yawn-free read for laymen should be regarded as a substitute for prompt and expert professional advice. Employment law is complex and some points have to be explained in a simplified form. Furthermore, the rules are subject to continual change; the references here are to developments reported up to 1 August 1990.

This book urges readers to take adequate steps to protect themselves. Self-protection is not the same as selfishness. Getting the best deal from your employer will help you to give of your best *for* your employer. Too many executives work in an atmosphere which makes them feel isolated and on the defensive. If the guidance offered here helps you to feel more secure, it will have served a useful purpose. Only if you enjoy reasonable peace of mind can you concentrate wholeheartedly on making your job a success.

Chapter 1

Taking Up a Job

1.1 Preliminaries

It is never too soon to start thinking about how to get the best deal from your employer. Even before you start a new job, there are several positive steps which you can take.

Job advertisements
You may first learn of a job through an advertisement in a newspaper or magazine. That advertisement will have been designed to attract interest, not only outlining what is on offer, but also seeking to project a suitable corporate image. When following it up, you need to check whether the promises correspond with reality.

Keep a copy of the advertisement. Dispose of it only when you lose interest in taking up the job, not before. If it influences you to join the company concerned, its importance may continue long after you actually start work. Court decisions have shown that the contents of a job advertisement may have a bearing on your legal rights. This is because, all too often, the details of an executive's employment are not adequately thought through at the right time, before the job begins. How to avoid this problem will be discussed later, but it is probably inevitable that there will sometimes be a degree of uncertainty.

There are several possible explanations for confusion about your precise position in law, including:

- a failure at the outset to anticipate the way in which circumstances may change in the future;
- ambiguity in the early correspondence and discussions;
- inconsistencies within, or omissions from, the wording of contract documents.

The initial advertisement may be relevant even if you later sign a written employment contract. One example is if the advertisement states that promotion to the board of directors will occur within two years, but your service agreement is silent on that issue and the hoped-for elevation does not take place. You might be able to establish that the company has broken its obligations to you and that you are entitled to financial compensation.

In disputes between companies and executives, courts and tribunals often have to ask themselves what the real agreement was between the parties. Any document that can help them to identify the precise terms of the deal is potentially important. That is one good reason why you should start your own job file – see Chapter 8 – and why the advertisement should be one of the first items in it.

Employment agencies
Many executives use the services of employment agencies. A formidable array of regulations controls the activities of such organisations, which are licensed by the Department of Employment. Agencies are prohibited from charging fees to employees for finding or attempting to find them jobs. They make their money from employer clients.

When giving your personal details to an agency, make it clear if there is any confidential information which should not be disclosed without your consent, and confirm that instruction in writing, keeping a copy for future reference. You may, for instance, be anxious to ensure that your interest in moving elsewhere does not become widely known in your particular industry or reach the ears of your present employer. If, despite your request, an agency does reveal private facts about you and you suffer loss as a result, you might be able to claim compensation from that agency. Such revelations are fortunately rare.

Initial correspondence and discussions
Years after you begin a new job, you may find that your legal rights in the event of a dispute with your company depend upon what was said and done before you originally joined. It is vital that your application for the post, your curriculum vitae and any letters that you write are accurate. This will not only help you to land the job but also tend to reduce the risk of your entering into a contract on unsuitable terms. Again, you should preserve copies of all documents in your personal job file. It is also a good idea to note down telephone conversations and points mentioned at interviews with

your prospective employers, so that a correct record exists if your memory of promises made is one day challenged.

A vague or careless approach can prove very costly. There is no better demonstration of this than the case of *Deeley v British Rail Engineering* (1980). Mr Deeley responded to an advertisement for a sales manager (export). He was appointed and worked both in the UK and overseas until his doctor advised him, following a period of illness, not to work abroad for 12 months. His employer offered him the position of senior sales engineer (railway equipment) dealing with domestic sales. He refused this job and was then dismissed.

When the dispute came before the Court of Appeal, the question was whether Mr Deeley could, under his contract, be transferred from the export side to the domestic post. All correspondence before the job was offered referred to 'export'. The offer letter, however, simply concerned the job of 'sales engineer'. Mr Deeley wrote to accept and just headed his letter 'sales engineer'. In the light of that, the judgment was that the earlier references specifically to an 'export' position had been superseded.

It is plain from the Court of Appeal's reasoning that judges will look closely at your early correspondence and discussions, when appropriate, to find out what was agreed. The whole factual background may be relevant. Mr Deeley was no doubt dismayed to learn that, in law, he had drifted into a contract that differed in a key respect from that which he and the company had originally envisaged. Yet it was easily done. This underlines the need for you to ensure that, at all times, what you say is exactly what you mean.

1.2 The employer's freedom to recruit

Traditionally, employers had a free hand in deciding whom they would or would not hire. The classic statement of the law came from Lord Davey in 1898:

> An employer may refuse to employ ... for the most mistaken, capricious, malicious or morally reprehensible motives that can be conceived, but the employee has no right of action against him.

Although a large measure of discretion still exists in the recruitment process, there are now legal constraints of varying importance. Most significant are the laws against discrimination on the grounds of race or sex. The operation of the rules in these areas (which are outlined in Chapter 9) is overseen by the Commission for Racial Equality and the Equal Opportunities Commission.

1.3 Are you an employee or self-employed?

You must at some stage make a choice between taking up employment and working on a self-employed basis. Your decision has a crucial effect upon your legal rights and obligations as a whole – not just upon your tax position. Employees have numerous potentially valuable entitlements which do not apply to the self-employed. They include statutory rights:

1. to minimum notice of the ending of the job and, sometimes, to minimum payments during that notice period;
2. to redundancy pay;
3. not to be unfairly dismissed.

The choice is often far from being clear-cut. It is, too, surprisingly difficult in many cases to draw the line between employment status and being one's own boss. Nevertheless, it is essential for you to know into which category you fall.

Unfortunately, the courts have been unable to develop a simple and comprehensive test for differentiating between a contract of service (ie for an employee) and a contract for services (ie in respect of a self-employed, independent person). The law reports are crowded with cases on the subject, but they provide useful pointers rather than an all-embracing solution.

Whether or not you work under the control of someone else – as regards both what you do and how you do it – might be relevant. But, realistically, if you occupy a senior executive post, the extent of your employer's control over your day-to-day activities is probably limited in practice. As an alternative, the courts sometimes ask whether the work done is performed as an integral part of the business or not; yet this so-called 'organisational' test raises as many questions as it answers.

It is usually better to start by looking at all the different aspects of the relationship between the company and the individual. For example, it will frequently be worth considering whether you are:

(a) paid wages or salary;
(b) paid during sickness absence;
(c) paid during holidays;
(d) a member of the company pension scheme;
(e) subject to disciplinary rules and procedures;
(f) prohibited from working for other employers;
(g) entitled to decline to work;

(h) taxed as an employee;
(i) regarded by both your employer and yourself as employed (eg in the terms of the written contract);
(j) responsible for employing your own assistants;
(k) responsible for some or all of the financial or commercial risk of the enterprise.

In many cases, there will be in the same relationship some factors apparently inconsistent with employment status and others which seem to preclude self-employment. The relative weight which any particular consideration carries will depend upon the circumstances. In any event, it is probably impossible to draw up a list of criteria which is truly exhaustive.

An agreement between your employer and yourself about your legal position may be overridden by the courts if it ignores what actually happens. The intention of the parties is, however, sometimes influential, especially if their agreement on the relationship clarifies what is in other respects ambiguous.

Strangely, the answer to a question about your legal status may vary with the reason for asking it. A person who is taxable on a self-employed basis may have the right of an employee to claim unfair dismissal.

This extraordinary state of affairs was examined by the Court of Appeal in the case of *Young and Woods Ltd v West* (1980). When Mr West joined the company he was offered alternative methods of payment, either as an employee or as self-employed. He opted for the latter. Income tax was therefore not deducted from his pay, he was responsible for his own National Insurance contributions and he received no holiday or sick pay. The Inland Revenue did not object to this arrangement.

Despite all that, the Court of Appeal decided that in law he was an employee. He was therefore not debarred from complaining to an industrial tribunal when the company dispensed with his services. The judgment was clearly geared to ensuring, as a matter of public policy, that an employer should not be allowed to dodge his statutory responsibilities by inducing a worker to give up his employment status in return for short-term financial gain. Modern employment law sets out stringent limits on the circumstances in which employees can 'contract out' of their rights.

Do not think that this means that you can always have your cake and eat it, enjoying both tax advantages and job security. The Court of Appeal indicated that it might be appropriate for the Inland Revenue to look at the matter again. Mr West's victory may therefore have proved hollow and indeed expensive.

To summarise, spending time and money on highly artificial contract arrangements is apt to be counter-productive in the long run. The courts are more interested in the reality of your legal position than in helping you to get the best of all possible worlds.

1.4 Directorships

If you are offered a directorship, you should ascertain exactly what it entails. In many companies, the title 'director' is used as a courtesy and has little practical or legal significance.

If, however, you are to take a seat on the board and become a director in the full sense, your particulars should be registered at Companies House. It is vital for you to familiarise yourself with all the attendant powers and duties under company law; these are matters which fall outside the scope of this book. You also need to make sure that your employment rights are adequately secured.

While a company director can be, and often is, an employee, that is not automatically the case. In *Albert J Parsons & Sons Ltd v Parsons* (1979), for instance, a full-time working director was considered by the Court of Appeal not to have employment rights. He was paid directors' fees rather than a salary and had not been treated as an employee for National Insurance purposes. Furthermore, there had been no attempt to comply with the requirement of the Companies Act that a company should keep at its registered office a copy of each director's written service agreement and a memorandum of the terms of all those directors' service agreements which are not themselves in writing. Mr Parsons was one of three brothers working in a family business and one can therefore imagine that he was surprised as well as dismayed by the court's decision.

As well as avoiding the traps into which Mr Parsons fell, it will also be wise to check that your salary is formally approved by resolution of the board and perhaps more importantly that, if your contract is to run for more than five years, it receives prior approval from the shareholders in accordance with company law.

1.5 Accepting an offer

Your contract of employment will usually come into existence when you unequivocally accept an offer of a job. The deal will then be struck. While you will normally accept by word of mouth or by letter, if you simply turn up on the appointed day and start work, your acceptance will be inferred from your conduct.

When you receive an offer and have all the information you need to decide whether or not to accept, it is wise not to delay too long in your response. An offer of work can normally be withdrawn at any time until it is accepted. This is perhaps worth remembering when you wonder about the possibility of haggling further, for example over salary or benefits.

If you accept a job, subject to one or more conditions which have not yet been agreed, the legal interpretation is that you are making a counter-offer, which destroys the effect of the offer made to you. The company may agree to your proposal, reject it or make a revised offer.

In the case of a revised offer, there will be a contract if you accept the terms which are now on the table. Your acceptance may be inferred if you start work without raising objections to the new offer.

Be wary about beginning a job before the negotiations have ended. This happens quite often, sometimes with unsatisfactory results from the employee's point of view. Once you take up a new post you have crossed the Rubicon. Your bargaining strength will almost inevitably be diminished. If the company then refuses to budge any further, you may be forced to choose between unsatisfactory terms and leaving straight away.

Another risk, which may not seem serious at the time but which may ultimately have expensive consequences, is that negotiations may just fizzle out if you start a job before all the details have been agreed. Later, when it matters, you might find it very difficult to identify exactly what the terms of your contractual deal really are. Whatever the pressure, therefore, you should make every effort to ensure that no major issue is unresolved at the stage when you make your move.

The job offer may be conditional, ie subject to receipt of references which satisfy your new employer. Whether the condition is simple or complicated, the company will not be bound to go through with the offer if that condition is not fulfilled. This might occur, perhaps, if the references are not considered 'satisfactory' – a point on which, in practice, an employer will have a considerable amount of discretion.

1.6 Changing your mind

What happens if, later on, you change your mind about joining a prospective employer or, even worse, he eventually decides not to let you start work?

In theory, the legal position is straightforward if a contract has been formed. You or, as the case may be, your employer can sue for compensation if the contract is broken, although neither side can insist that the agreement be carried out against the other's will. The amount that can be claimed is generally the amount of reasonably foreseeable loss that has been suffered; the principles in this area are further discussed in Chapter 18.

In practice, employers who are disappointed in this way tend simply to write it off to experience. Yet while they seldom resort to litigation, you cannot rule out the possibility altogether. Certainly, if you are contemplating a last-minute change of mind, it would be prudent to seek professional advice.

Sometimes it will not be clear whether or not a contract exists. If you have been badly let down in confused circumstances, all is not necessarily lost. A group of employees who were similarly treated a few years ago succeeded in legal action against employers who vigorously denied that there was a binding deal.

The men concerned were insulation engineers who were told that highly paid jobs were available at Sullom Voe. They knew that the work would last for at least six months and that on arrival they would be required to undergo a medical examination and sign a contract. They applied for the jobs and were told they were acceptable and that it was in order for them to resign from their current jobs. Before the men left for the Shetlands, though, the company bowed to union pressure and told them that, 'due to circumstances beyond our control we are no longer able to employ you'.

Intriguingly, the High Court of Northern Ireland ruled in *Gill and others v Cape Contracts Ltd* (1985) that, as the men had given up their jobs in reliance on the promises made by the company, they were entitled to compensation when those promises were broken. Thus, even if you do not have a contract of employment in the orthodox sense, it is possible for you and your prospective employer to become subject to legally binding rights and duties while your negotiations are still ongoing. The Gill case is therefore another reminder that both sides should conduct their preliminary discussions with care.

1.7 Are you breaking an existing contract?

A job offer may depend upon your starting work by a specified date. Even it is does not, your prospective employer will usually be keen for you to start in the near future.

Both of you need to be wary. If you leave your old job without giving proper notice under your contract, your disgruntled former employers may take reprisals through litigation.

The first safety measure is for you to check what your notice obligation is; the law on this topic is dealt with in Chapter 6. If the notice period is short, the odds are that very few problems will arise. If it is lengthy, you may have to rely to an extent on your present employer's goodwill. Frank discussion with him is often the best course. He may not object too strongly to your early departure, on the assumption that there is little to be gained from keeping a demotivated executive chained to his desk. Even if he hates to see you go, he may be realistic enough to recognise a *fait accompli*.

He may bargain over your leaving terms, perhaps asking you to waive some of your contractual rights in return for being allowed to start the new job sooner than would otherwise be possible. If you eventually arrive at an acceptable deal, it makes sense to document the agreement in writing.

If you walk out without an arrangement to commute your notice period, your former employer will almost certainly find it impossible to force you to return against your wishes by taking out a law suit. He may, however, obtain an injunction, ie a court order, preventing you from taking up your new post. This kind of action will cost him time and money, so it is most likely to be used if you are joining a rival firm and he fears the consequences.

You cannot altogether rule out the possibility that you may be sued for damages for breaking your contract, though few employers actually pursue this line of attack. Those who do may seek compensation for the financial loss that they have suffered, including the cost of hiring replacement staff.

Another risk is that you may face legal action if you commit a breach of an express or implied constraint on your future conduct; this complex but important topic is discussed further in Chapters 5 and 21.

Your new employers may be sued for inducing you to break your contract. Again, an injunction might be sought to prevent them from continuing the inducement and there could also be a claim for compensation. It goes without saying that you should warn them in advance of your existing notice commitment and about your former employers' likely reaction to the news that you are leaving.

Don't take chances unnecessarily. If you are being persuaded to break your contract, make sure that your new employers agree to indemnify you against costs of any kind that you may incur as a result. Make sure the indemnity is confirmed in writing and is legally enforceable. If they want you badly enough to urge you to risk legal action, they should not jib at such an undertaking.

1.8 Probationary periods

Although personnel managers may find it provides a useful framework for monitoring the performance of new recruits, the concept of a probationary period after starting work now has little legal significance.

If you begin a new job with an employer not associated (in the technical legal sense) with your previous company, the law requires you to build up a two-year period of continuous employment before you are eligible for unfair dismissal rights. Although there are one or two exceptions to this basic rule (for example, there is no qualifying period in the case of some dismissals for trade union-related reasons), they are seldom relevant to business executives.

In effect, therefore, your employer can dismiss you unfairly before the two-year period is up and your only redress (if any) will be a claim under your contract. In this respect, the length of any specified probationary period might be relevant if you could argue that it was part of the agreement that you be allowed to work it out or at least be paid up until it came to an end.

1.9 Illegal agreements

Courts and tribunals refuse to allow people to enforce any rights that they may have under a contract that is tainted by illegality. Employees discover this to their cost when, for example, they seek to claim unfair dismissal or notice pay and it turns out that they had wrongly agreed with their employers that part of their salary should be paid tax-free. Applying this principle can have severe effects: senior and long-serving employees may forfeit immensely valuable rights, even when the fiddles that they have indulged in have only involved insignificant sums of money.

The moral is clear. Never, in any circumstances, allow yourself to be talked into entering an illegal arrangement either before your employment begins or at a later date. The law reports contain many sad cases of those who have done so and who have lived to regret it.

Chapter 2

Your Employment Contract

2.1 The framework

Your employment contract is important. It should reflect the deal you have struck with your employer. There is a good deal of sense in Sam Goldwyn's famous remark that a verbal contract isn't worth the paper it is written on. Even so, English law has never laid down a general rule that a business executive's employment contract should be in writing. Many are not.

The fundamental problem with verbal agreements is that there may, one day, be a dispute about what was actually said. It is highly desirable for the terms to be properly documented. Moreover, various matters do, by law, have to be put in writing; these are discussed later.

Do not think, though, that the mere act of putting pen to paper is enough in itself. If what is written down is vague or incoherent, the whole exercise will prove fruitless. Another danger is that, over a period of time, a number of documents may come into being which contradict each other. Sorting out the terms that did in fact apply to your job at any particular stage may, if you are not careful, prove to be a Herculean task.

Chapter 1 showed how the terms of an employment contract may arise in the most haphazard way. If you fail to keep your wits about you and find yourself committed to an unsatisfactory agreement, the law may not provide an adequate safety net. Bear in mind that, if a court is asked to rule on your contract position, it will analyse the agreed terms in a formal way and not necessarily reach a conclusion that you would regard as 'fair' or as in the spirit of your deal with the company.

Because the recruitment process is so often complex, there is no golden rule about when all the terms of the employment contract come into being. We have seen that, although a job offer may supersede earlier correspondence, it does not always destroy the legal effect of everything that has taken place earlier. Equally, points which are agreed and documents that are drawn up later may have an important bearing upon your rights and duties. For instance, the offer may be unclear or inadequate in some vital respects and it may be some weeks or months before key issues are finally clarified.

Even if you take the precaution of making sure that the terms of your agreement have been recorded clearly and efficiently, that is not the end of the story. No single document, however long, is likely to cover every eventuality.

If there are gaps, they may be filled in a number of ways. First, if you are a member of a recognised trade union, terms from a collective agreement between your union and the company may be included in your personal contract. Even if the terms are not legally binding on your union, as is often the case, it is possible for them to be binding as between your employer and yourself.

Second, legislation may imply a term into your contract. Thus every contract is now deemed to include an 'equality clause'. This means that where you are employed on:

1. like work; or
2. work rated as equivalent; or
3. work of equal value;

to that of a person of the opposite sex in the same employment, then any contract term that is or becomes less favourable to you is modified, so that it is no longer unfavourable.

Finally, the courts will imply certain terms into your contract. In practice, the fewer terms which are specifically agreed, the more likely it is that the courts will imply a wide range of terms into your agreement. This may have a crucial effect on the nature of your deal with your employer.

2.2 Letters of appointment

Many business executives are appointed by letter. In an ideal world, all letters of appointment would be clear and comprehensive. In reality, they are frequently neither.

Read your letter of appointment slowly and critically as soon as you receive it, taking nothing for granted. The discipline of composing it may have brought management's attention to new points included, or confirm or amend the particulars or substitute new ones. If your employment has come to an end, you must make your complaint within three months of the termination date.

Frankly, you will seldom wish to bother. In fact, hardly anyone does, because the law has so few teeth in this area. The tribunal cannot fine an employer who fails to comply with his statutory duty, nor can it bring to book an employer who fails to honour the written particulars – another reason why you should make sure that your terms are clearly agreed in writing at the outset.

The legal status of a written statement

Contrary to widespread belief, a written statement of particulars of employment 'is not the contract; it is not even conclusive evidence of the contract'.

These were the words of the Court of Appeal when it confirmed that a statutory statement is, in law, simply very strong *prima facie* evidence of what the terms of an employment contract are. Thus, an employer who issues a written statement will have trouble persuading a court that the actual terms of the contract differed from those included in the statement.

You might find it easier to challenge the validity of the statutory statement, should you ever need to do so. Even if you sign it to acknowledge receipt, a court will not always interpret that signature as confirmation that the statement contains terms which legally bind you. It will, though, be different if you have signed to confirm that you accept the statement as having the effect of a contract.

This is not just an academic distinction. In *Jones v Associated Tunnelling Co Ltd* (1981), written statements had provided, for four years, that Mr Jones might be required 'to transfer from one site to another on the instruction of the employer'. He had signed the statement acknowledging receipt.

Nevertheless, the Employment Appeal Tribunal was prepared to imply into Mr Jones's contract a term which contradicted the written statement. It considered that the correct implied term was that the company had the right to transfer Mr Jones 'to any place within reasonable commuting reach of his home'. Although Mr Jones had not objected to the written statement which suggested that he could be asked to work over a wide geographic area, this was not considered to be too significant because at the time the statements were issued, they had no immediate practical importance for him.

It pays to read the small print of any statement that is issued to you. In particular, if you are asked to sign a copy, check that this does not mean that you are inadvertently agreeing to terms which have not been the subject of proper discussion and which, in your opinion, form no part of the deal. If it becomes clear that you are at odds with your employer, even if only about a minor matter, try to resolve the matter promptly, before it assumes undue importance. Do not rely on enjoying the same success in litigation as Mr Jones.

2.4 Service agreements and back-up documents

A custom has grown up of referring to written employment contracts relating to business executives as service agreements. There is no special magic in this expression; 'service agreement' is another way of saying 'contract of employment'.

Nowadays, many service agreements are long and complex. A typical example is set out in Appendix 1. Like many such agreements, it is broadly drafted in a number of key respects and is peppered with bits of legal jargon. If you are not clear about the precise meaning of such a document, it is wise to take professional advice before you sign.

Company handbooks

Many companies issue handbooks as a means of communication with their employees and, perhaps, to help induction training. Handbooks often contain the points normally found in written statements of particulars, but with additional coverage of matters such as:

1. maternity rights;
2. health and safety rules;
3. time-off rights;
4. any special amenities and services, such as the right to purchase company products at concessionary rates;
5. any policy on equal opportunities, ie to the effect that employees will be treated equally, regardless of sex, race, age or physical disability.

Study the contents carefully.

Disciplinary rules and procedures

The Advisory, Conciliation and Arbitration Service (ACAS) has long recommended that employers should issue written disciplinary rules and procedures. This helps to promote fairness and consistency in handling individual employment problems.

The contents of disciplinary rules and procedures are infinitely variable, but a number of key principles are outlined in the ACAS Code of Practice on disciplinary practice and procedures. It emphasises that, among other matters, procedures should:

(a) indicate the disciplinary actions which may be taken;
(b) provide for individuals to be informed of the complaints against them and to be given an opportunity to state their case before decisions are reached;
(c) give individuals the right to be accompanied at disciplinary interviews;
(d) ensure that, except for gross misconduct, no employees are dismissed for a first breach of discipline;
(e) ensure that individuals are given an explanation of any penalty imposed.

Whether or not any written disciplinary rules are specifically said to form part of your contract, you should familiarise yourself with them. If you break the rules, your job could be at risk (see Chapter 12).

2.5 Implied terms

Because no one can think of everything, the courts sometimes have to imply terms into contracts. They have been more willing to do so where employment contracts are concerned than in the case of other agreements.

Traditionally, judges looked at the intention of the parties at the time that they entered into a contract. They would imply terms into that contract only:

1. where it was necessary in order to make the contract work; or
2. where the term to be implied was so obvious that, had the parties been asked whether they would both have agreed to it, they would both have said, 'Of course!'

In employment cases during the past few years, there has been a more liberal approach. Courts have implied terms simply where it has seemed reasonable to do so, having regard to the actions of the employer and employee during the existence of the contract. One result of this attitude has been increasing uncertainty about when a term will or will not be implied.

A case dealing with sick pay rights illustrates the modern trend. In *Mears v Safecar Security Ltd* (1982), the Court of Appeal accepted that it would be normal to imply a term that wages would be paid when employees were absent because of sickness. There would be no such presumption, though, where it was inconsistent with the actions of the parties and the surrounding circumstances during the period of employment.

Similarly, it seems that an employer's freedom to discipline his employees for alleged offences may be subject to an important implied constraint. In *BBC v Beckett* (1983), the BBC disciplined an employee by demoting him in accordance with a disciplinary process which formed part of his employment contract. The Employment Appeal Tribunal said that the ability of an employer to act in accordance with express terms was limited because there was an implied agreement that a punishment would not be inflicted which was 'grossly out of proportion to the offence'.

Because the courts have allowed themselves some latitude in this area, predicting which terms will be implied into a contract is not always straightforward. However, you can safely assume that, even if nothing is put in writing or if the contract does not deal with the point, you will be expected:

(a) to obey reasonable orders given by an authorised superior;
(b) to exercise reasonable care and skill;
(c) to act in good faith towards your employer.

Conversely, your employer is under an implied duty not to do anything likely to destroy the relationship of confidence between you.

Implied contract terms assume particular significance if you feel that you are being unjustly treated. In order to be able to launch a constructive dismissal claim, for instance, you need to be able to show that your contract has been broken by your employer. One way of doing so is to argue that the implied obligation of mutual trust and confidence has been breached. This idea is explored more fully in Chapter 15.

Sometimes you will have no option but to rely on terms which you believe should be implied into your contract. You will sleep more easily, however, if you keep these occasions to a minimum. Thrash out your deal with your employer in as much detail as possible.

Chapter 3

Checking the Basics

3.1 The need to check

Psychologically, and also for practical reasons, the best time to iron out any uncertainties about the terms under which you are to work is before your job begins. There is, of course, often a temptation to put off sorting out the detail once you have reached agreement on status, salary and benefits. You may be disinclined to rock the boat by pressing for clarification of other terms. Management may seem equally relaxed about the whole exercise, promising to 'get round to it later'. As time passes, everyone becomes so busy that the absence of a comprehensive document is forgotten.

Do not fall into this trap. The longer you leave it, the harder it is likely to be to resolve points of doubt in a satisfactory way. If important matters remain unresolved, you could find to your cost that if a dispute does eventually arise, your legal position is more vulnerable than you realised. Your deal may even turn out to be quite different from what you thought. Hiring a suitably experienced lawyer to advise you on what exactly should go into your contract is almost always much easier and cheaper in the long run than retaining his services when the prospect of a court battle looms.

Issues that, on the surface, seem so straightforward as not to be worthy of a second thought may prove, when the crunch comes, to be vital. Even something as apparently obvious as the question of which legal system applies to your contract may lead to unexpected problems if, for example, you work for a company based overseas. The difference between relying on the company's standard notice terms and negotiating your own, much longer entitlement to notice could be quantified in tens of thousands of pounds if one day you are asked to leave. These matters are discussed more fully in Chapters 6 and 7.

So, even in the honeymoon period after you have been offered and have accepted an exciting new job, you should take nothing for granted. To do so might turn out to be the worst career mistake that you ever make.

3.2 Who are you working for?

You need to know who your employer is. This sounds crashingly obvious, but even so, in a significant minority of cases, and despite the fact that the information should be contained in the statutory statement, some executives simply do not know the precise identity of their employer.

This matters because your job rights may be of little value if you are not sure whom to sue if these rights are infringed or if the legal entity that you are entitled to sue becomes insolvent or ceases to exist.

Working within a group of companies
Usually, the problem arises within a corporate group. The holding company may be a substantial and well-known organisation, but one or two of its subsidiaries might be more recently established, with a tiny issued share capital and liable to be wrapped up with little or no warning once they have served their commercial purposes. In the eyes of the law, and with only a few exceptions, each limited company is regarded as a separate body. Trying to claim against one organisation for the misdeeds of another is hazardous.

Confusion sometimes arises at the outset concerning which company is making the job offer. For example, you may respond to an advertisement referring to the holding company, be interviewed at the office of its marketing subsidiary by an external management consultant, receive a letter of appointment from the local regional office and be paid through a computer system operated by another member of the group that you had never previously heard of. Disentangling this kind of complexity in a courtroom several years later is apt to be as expensive as it is tricky.

Your objectives should therefore be twofold. First, you need to ensure that you are employed by the branch of the organisation that is appropriate to your particular place in the management structure. Second, and even more important, you need to be confident that you are working for a business of substance.

Secondment

Secondment is another potential source of complications. Whether you are asked to work for a business other than your employer's from the start of your job or at a later stage, you ought, even if you are agreeable, to find out:

1. the exact identity of the business to which you are being seconded;
2. the purpose of the secondment;
3. how long it will last and, if it may become permanent, in what circumstances;
4. whether any of your normal contract terms are affected at all and, if so, how;
5. whether there is any guarantee that your original job will still be waiting for you when the secondment ends.

As ever, it is prudent to get the deal set down in writing.

Business sales

For centuries, the law regarded the employment relationship as fundamentally a personal one. This principle has now been encroached upon, albeit in the hope of enhancing overall job security. Since 1982, people working for an employer whose business is sold to someone else have been transferred automatically to work for the purchaser. This is the effect of the Transfer of Undertakings (Protection of Employment) Regulations of 1981, a measure designed to implement the EC Directive. Introduced with a marked lack of enthusiasm by Margaret Thatcher's government, the detailed rules are intricate and often hard to interpret.

The Regulations apply to:

1. a transfer of an undertaking (but not mere share sales); where
2. the undertaking or part of it that is transferred is situated in the UK at the time of the transfer; and it is
3. run as a commercial venture.

An 'undertaking' includes any trade or business. Whether there is a transfer of an undertaking will depend on the facts, but it will often involve the transfer of goodwill, such as the order book and the clients, as well as, usually, a sale of the assets.

If you are employed in an undertaking immediately before it is transferred, you will be transferred automatically to work in the purchaser's business. If, as a result of the change-over, you lose your job, you may have the right to claim unfair dismissal.

Experience shows that many employees in this situation are unaware of their rights. Again, you may find it worthwhile to invest in expert legal advice about your position so that you know where you stand should you have to negotiate a new deal, for instance following the takeover of the business in which you have been working.

3.3 When does your job begin?

Many of your rights under modern employment law depend upon your having built up a specified minimum period of 'continuous employment'. The concept of continuous employment therefore has a great deal of practical importance. How long you have been continuously employed for can, furthermore, be highly relevant if ever you have to assess the value of a termination package offered by your employers.

The rules in this area are set out in the Consolidation Act. They are elaborate and only a brief overview of some of the main points can be given here. Suffice it to say that, as so often happens where legal matters are concerned, the position is less straightforward than you might think.

Generally, your period of continuous employment begins on your first day at work. This means in practice the date upon which your contract requires you to start working (which may not be quite the same as the day when you first sit behind your desk, for example if you fall ill and are unable to begin on the agreed commencement date). Exceptionally, for the purposes of the redundancy payment scheme only, the period can begin no earlier than your eighteenth birthday.

You can count as part of your continuous period any week in which you actually work for 16 hours or more in which your contract normally involves your working for 16 hours or more, even if you worked less, for example because of sickness. If you have been continuously employed for five years or more, you can count weeks when your contract normally involved working for less than 16, but at least eight hours per week.

Any week during which you were away because of a 'temporary cessation of work' may count towards your continuous period. This may be relevant if you work on a seasonal basis or if the nature of your job entails a succession of short-term, intermittent contracts, as is the case with some teachers and lecturers who are just employed for the academic year.

In deciding whether the cessation is only temporary, it might be relevant to look at:

1. the type of job;
2. the length of prior and subsequent service;
3. the duration of the break;
4. what was said when the break occurred;
5. what was said when the job began.

Although continuous employment normally means time spent working for a single employer, this is not always so. If there is a transfer of an undertaking, as described above for example, your period of work for the old business will be added to your period of employment with the purchaser.

If you work within a corporate group, your period of continuous employment will not be broken if you move from one 'associated employer' to another. This would be the case if you work for two or more companies, both of which are controlled (in the terms of voting rights) by the same individual or organisation, such as two subsidiaries of the same holding company.

In the early stages of a new job, keep in mind the vital significance of accumulating a sufficient period of employment. If things go wrong, for instance, it might be vital for you to resist the temptation to confront management with ultimatums until you are sure that you have the safety net (however limited) of having acquired the right to complain to an industrial tribunal if, as a result, you are sacked.

3.4 Job title and duties

Most employers like to adopt a flexible approach as regards the duties that they can ask you to perform. Although, as we have seen, the statutory statement should include your job title, you have no legal right to a job description.

A short job title will not normally restrict the range of tasks that you can be asked to perform to a very great extent. Thus, a tribunal could hold that the title of 'engineer' impliedly covers a wide variety of duties associated with the basic work of being an engineer. Even so, the Employment Appeal Tribunal has suggested that when a title is to be widely interpreted, an employee should be told.

From your point of view, the more information that you have about what is expected of you, the better. First, having a clear understanding of the company's requirements is essential if you are to give of your best. Second, if you are unfairly blamed for failing to achieve what, in reality, you were never asked to do, you will want to have a document to point to in your defence. Third, if you are ordered to carry out some task which plainly falls outside your job description, being able to justify a refusal to comply might mean the difference between saving your job and facing a fair dismissal (see Chapter 12).

As will emerge in later chapters, the nature of your duties will have other, potentially far-reaching implications. They may have a bearing on the extent of your legal rights in any invention you make or any design, drawing or computer program that you create (see Chapter 5). They could affect your fate if your employer ever finds it necessary to impose redundancies (see Chapter 13). Finally, they could also be relevant if you feel that your job is being downgraded and wish to consider pursuing a constructive dismissal claim (see Chapter 15).

So there is much to be said in favour of pressing your employer to give you a comprehensive job description. Provided that it is realistic and accurate, there will seldom be any cause to object if its contents are built into your employment contract. It is, after all, part of the deal between you and the company.

3.5 Place of work

Disputes about job location crop up from time to time. Frequently, they arise from a failure to agree on the appropriate place or places of work when the contract is drawn up. This is something which, in the interests of both the company and yourself, should normally be dealt with clearly and in writing.

It is not enough for you to be confident that, usually, you will be working from a single base which is close enough to home. You should also think about the following issues:

1. Can you be moved elsewhere and, if so, how much notice will you be given of any proposed move?
2. How far away from your present place of work can you be moved?
3. Are you entitled to decline to move?
4. If so, are you eligible for redundancy rights (see Chapter 13)?
5. Are you able to negotiate improved pay or benefits as a condition of moving?

A certain amount of flexibility may be implied in many jobs even if there is no express 'mobility clause'. The Employment Appeal Tribunal has said that:

> One would have thought that an employee cannot refuse justifiably to continue to work for his employers merely because the employers move the office to a new building down the street. But when it comes to moving to a different town or to a different quarter of the same town, or even a few miles away in the same town, different considerations may apply.

In another case, it was decided that a manageress of an office in London was employed to work anywhere in central London, different parts of which were equally accessible to her by public transport. An implied term of this sort, along the lines indicated in Chapter 2, that one may be required to work anywhere within reasonable commuting distance of home, will often be appropriate.

All the same, each case must be judged individually; there is no hard and fast rule. The courts may look at the nature of the job, a senior executive in a large company being expected to be more mobile than his secretary. Other terms of the contract, such as an express right to be reimbursed in respect of travelling expenses and hotel costs, may also be pointers towards there being a significant degree of mobility.

There is much to be said for removing uncertainty by reaching a clear agreement about where you can and cannot be asked to work. It is only sensible, though, to recognise that occasionally, even when under the strict terms of the contract you cannot be forced to move, there may be no viable alternative. This might be the case if you face redundancy, or if you are in effect locked into your job by a premium salary level that you cannot match elsewhere.

On the other hand, you should not forget the economics of house removal. If you live in an area where property prices are low, but your company has outlets in regions where they are high, it will be important to make sure that any mobility clause is supplemented by an agreement that the costs that you incur in moving will be borne (at least up to an agreed ceiling) by your company if you are asked to relocate.

Chapter 4

Pay and Benefits

4.1 The money side

Money isn't everything. All the same, you should not underrate the importance of sorting out financial matters when negotiating with your employers or prospective employers. There is seldom a good reason for failing to ensure that your entitlements are adequately recorded in writing.

Fringe benefits are often an important part of the overall remuneration package (or 'compensation package', to use a trendier but less strictly appropriate phrase). The kinds of benefit available take an almost infinite variety of forms. Much will depend upon the type of job in question. Again, it is advisable to iron out the details sooner rather than later.

One day, there could be an argument about whether you are legally entitled to some of the 'perks' that you take for granted. An example of such a dispute is examined in detail in Chapter 18. It is therefore important that a written agreement should spell out whether each and every benefit is discretionary or (if you can so arrange it) your contractual right.

In assessing the value of your overall remuneration, you need, of course, to take taxation into account. This book concentrates on the legal aspects of your job and does not attempt to explore tax matters in detail. It might be sensible to consult an accountant with expertise in the field of personal taxation who may be able to advise on the more efficient structuring of your total package.

A growing number of companies, mindful of skill shortage and demographic factors such as the ageing of the national work-force, are willing to offer a range of imaginative incentives, unheard of a few years ago, such as exotic holidays or a box at Brands Hatch. Indeed, we are told that the age of the executive compensation consultant has arrived. High fliers may wish to engage the services of a suitably experienced expert to help them strike the keenest possible deal.

4.2 'Golden' payments

Golden hellos, golden handcuffs and golden parachutes have become vogue phrases during the past few years. As so often with fashionable jargon, the precise meaning of the different concepts is apt to become confused.

Golden hellos

If your skills are in demand, you may be offered a cash inducement to join a new employer. 'Golden hellos', as they are now frequently called, may involve the payment of a one-off lump sum or instalment payments over a period of time, perhaps linked to the results that you achieve in your new employment

Your accountant may advise that, for tax reasons, the ideal would be for you to receive a lump sum, which is paid before your old job ends and which is not conditional upon your actually accepting the new position. In reality, it is hardly surprising that most employers are reluctant to take the risk that, if the inducement is not strictly linked to your joining them, you may simply bank the cash and decide not to move.

Companies are also keen, naturally enough, to make sure that if they pay handsomely to obtain executive skills, they will continue to retain the benefit of them for several years. You therefore need to check whether your job offer or contract provides that, if you leave before a specified date, you will have to reimburse the signing-on fee (and, if appropriate, any relocation expenses), either wholly or in part.

Golden handcuffs

In businesses where there is considerable mobility among employees, so-called 'golden handcuffs' have become popular.

Their purpose is to retain key executives and discourage them from succumbing to a golden hello. Such individuals are offered cash incentives to stay on, handcuffing them to their present employer in effect.

The tax treatment for handcuff payments may be open to debate, but generally sums paid will be taxable as income in the normal way. If the point becomes relevant, you should seek specific advice.

Golden parachutes
The phrase 'golden parachute' is frequently used in the USA. Here, it is sometimes treated as a synonym of 'golden handshake'. The two concepts are, however, better thought of as being distinct.

As is explained in Chapter 19, golden handshakes may carry tax advantages. Golden parachutes, on the other hand, are apt to be tax-inefficient.

Briefly, the parachute takes the form of a payment which the employment contract provides will be made in the event of the executive's job being terminated. It sounds like a neat idea, but if you have such a clause built into your agreement, you could find yourself being taxed on the whole sum, without the benefit of the relaxed rules on golden handshakes, if the worst happens. Seek expert advice on the wording of any such provision.

4.3 Salary

It goes almost without saying that you should take the precaution of reaching a clear agreement about your salary level before accepting a job offer. It is also often desirable to go further and try to obtain some firm commitment about salary increases in the future.

Keep in mind that you cannot compel your employer to agree to vary the terms of your employment contract. This means that, normally, it will not be possible to argue that you have a legal right to a pay rise if the contract is silent on that point. Just conceivably, if colleagues of a similar status in the organisation receive pay increases but you do not, you might be able to argue that you have been treated 'arbitrarily, capriciously or inequitably' and that you have been constructively dismissed (see Chapter 15). Suffice it to say here that for a senior executive to make such a claim would be something of a long shot.

So it may be attractive to build into your agreement a provision dealing with the circumstances in which you will be eligible for an uplift in salary. A vaguely worded clause, however, such as one in which your employer undertakes to 'review' your salary on an annual basis, but says no more, might make you feel better, but will often be of little practical value.

Index-linking

One possible solution is for your salary to be index-linked. Any index chosen should be:

1. prepared by a reputable, independent organisation;
2. recalculated regularly; and
3. reasonably accessible.

A clause referring to such an index should, to be on the safe side, cater for:

(a) temporary suspension of publication;
(b) any change in the basis of calculation;
(c) publication ceasing.

The cost of living index, ie the Index of Retail Prices (RPI), is the one to which reference is usually made. Inflation-indexing seems fair enough, but remember that it is far from being a perfect way of rewarding effort. You may not maintain a comparable salary with that earned by others in similar jobs elsewhere. Furthermore, the increase in the RPI is a crude measure which will not accurately reflect the value of your personal contribution to the success of your company or its profitability. If you are a higher income earner, to increase your gross salary by the inflation rate may well not increase your net spending power, after tax, by the same amount.

You will probably feel happier, therefore, if any index-linking clause contained in your contact provides that the minimum pay rise will be in line with the increase in the chosen index, while the possibility remains of your being awarded a higher increase if the company's financial state permits.

4.4 Commission

If you are entitled to commission, for example on sales of company products, you need to know whether you will receive it as of right under the contract. If so, it will be helpful to have a clause included in your contract which makes the commission terms clear.

Among the points that may need to be covered are:

1. the basis of payment (for example, on sales orders obtained or those actually fulfilled);
2. the rate of payment;
3. when payment becomes due;
4. the intervals at which it is to be made.

4.5 Bonus

Bonuses may be paid for several different reasons. They might be one-off, discretionary payments or your contractual right. Again, you need to find out which.

Contractual bonuses are often linked to the amount of net profits in each financial year. Most clauses provide that the amount payable should be that certified by the company auditors. That may be non-negotiable, but you should at least study the definition of 'net profits' in order to assess the true potential worth of your entitlement.

4.6 Other payments

Check your contract to see that the position as regards any other payment is accurately documented. Typically, the following may be covered:

1. sick pay;
2. holiday pay;
3. relocation expenses if you are required to move pursuant to the terms of a mobility clause in your contract;
4. expenses incurred in performing your duties, ie reimbursement of moneys that you have paid out on the company's behalf.

While, as we saw in Chapter 2, you may have an implied right to sick pay, it is much better to reach express agreement. You will also have more peace of mind if your company participates in an insurance scheme which pays out to sick or disabled employees who are prevented from working, for the duration of their employment up to retirement.

4.7 Benefits

Motor car

Even if you are satisfied with the type of car provided to you by your employer, check who is responsible for expenses such as:

1. petrol;
2. maintenance and servicing;
3. taxation;
4. insurance.

Using a car may be integral to your job. But what happens if, for some reason, you are not carrying out your duties: are you entitled to retain the car for your exclusive private use?

This question arises most often – and most acrimoniously – when an executive given notice of dismissal is not required to work out his notice. If you are ever in that position, being able to point to a clause in your contract which makes it clear that you are entitled to keep the car until your employment eventually ends could be worth a great deal in hard cash terms. This point is perfectly illustrated by the case of *Shove v Downs Surgical plc* (1984), discussed in Chapter 18, where the value of the car benefit in a breach of contract case was judged to be £10,000.

Share incentive schemes

During the past decade or so, successive Chancellors of the Exchequer have tried to create a climate in which employers are encouraged to give their employees a stake in the business. The attraction of benefiting from tax concessions has caused share incentive schemes to become an increasingly common ingredient of executive remuneration packages.

There are various types of share incentives. Some require prior approval from the Inland Revenue. They include:

1. approved profit-sharing schemes;
2. approved share option schemes;
3. savings-related share option schemes.

The detailed rules applicable to the different types of scheme are complex and beyond the scope of this book. It is noteworthy that, usually, a company will not be able to compel you (even after you leave to join a competitor) to dispose of your shares. Bear in mind, however, that it can retain a general power to prevent you from selling to a purchaser of whom the directors do not approve and that, if you do move elsewhere, you will probably prefer to cash in the value of your shares.

Pension schemes

Pension rights are valuable. They are not always thought of as being as attractive a benefit as, say, a company car, but it is a mistake to underrate their importance. A pension is an investment in your future and that of your dependants.

Until recently, restrictions on the portability of pensions acted as a major disincentive to employee mobility. The legal rules used to mean that an executive who lost his job, even through no fault of his own, was often seriously disadvantaged in pension terms. Fortunately, these problems have been alleviated over the past few years, though not entirely solved.

You may wish to become a member of your employer's scheme, if there is one. Find out as much as you can about how it operates and what it is worth to you. As an alternative, you may prefer to take out a personal pension.

Contractual redundancy schemes

One can understand why few executives taking up a new job give too much thought to the possibility that one day they might be made redundant. Yet even a company which is highly profitable may have to make cut-backs at some future date. If your job is eventually rationalised out of existence, you will find that the strict rules on calculating the amount of statutory redundancy pay – discussed in Chapter 17 – probably mean that you are entitled to less than you would hope for.

Fortunately, many companies are prepared to offer redundant executives more than the legal minimum. A generous redundancy scheme is a welcome feature of an overall package of benefits.

Contractual rights in the event of redundancy vary from business to business, but may include:

1. an undertaking by the employer to 'top up' the statutory payment, for example by doubling, trebling or even quadrupling it;
2. an extended notice period;
3. help with retraining and/or out-placement counselling.

Other benefits

You may be able to persuade your employer to award you a number of other fringe benefits. These might include:

1. life assurance;
2. private health care;
3. free or subsidised accommodation;
4. cheap loans;
5. meal allowances;
6. home telephone charges;
7. professional subscriptions;
8. paternity leave;
9. sabbaticals.

Quite apart from their real value while your job lasts, these perks will, if built into your contract, enhance the value of your financial claims if you are ever faced with wrongful or unfair dismissal. Time spent negotiating their inclusion in the deal will prove to have been invested wisely.

Chapter 5

Restrictions on Your Freedom

5.1 What to watch for

Business life is competitive. Information, ideas and experience provide the key to success, not only in the area of up-to-the-minute technology, but in all industries, old and new. In your executive position, you are likely to come across manufacturing techniques, marketing strategies and other items of know-how which are commercially valuable.

When you enter into an employment contract, you become subject to a variety of restrictions as regards the use that you may make of the knowledge gained through your job. Even if you have no written contract, a number of constraints are implied by the common law.

Many employers find it necessary to impose additional, often far-reaching, restrictions in order to safeguard what they perceive as their legitimate business interests. Clause 12 of the sample agreement in Appendix 1 is an example; even more elaborate provisions are quite common. You may be asked to sign a service agreement containing a series of clauses, perhaps running on for several closely typed pages, which apparently put severe limits on your freedom of activity during and even after the job has ended.

You cannot afford not to give careful thought to the practical consequences before you respond to any such request. Simply for the chairman of the company to assure you that these are 'standard' requirements which apply to all senior employees is not sufficient. You need to weigh up whether you are destroying, or at least reducing, your value in the market-place should you wish in the future to move on, by agreeing to what is proposed. Try to take a long-term view. If you fail to do so, your deal may turn out eventually to be much less attractive than you thought.

Do not make the mistake of thinking that your employers will not wish or be able to insist that you abide by a set of tough restrictions once you have left. If your company has taken expert advice when having its contracts drawn up, you may discover that constraints have been included which are legally effective despite being tightly worded and, from your point of view, harsh.

Far better to grasp the nettle and argue over the scope of the clauses concerned on day one, before signing up, than at the time when you want to go but fear that your plans for the future contravene the small print of your agreement. Be warned. The law in this area is complex and continuing to evolve. This chapter offers only an outline. Specific professional advice is almost certain to be cheaper if you seek it sooner rather than later.

5.2 Documents and copyright

If your talents lie in the artistic or literary field, technical drawing or the development of computer programs, you will need to know the extent of your personal rights in the work that you create during your employment. If you do own part or all of it, does signing your service agreement entail signing away your ownership?

Copyright law is important here. It applies to a wide range of creative activities. For instance, after a period of debate, legislation has been passed so as to make it clear that computer software can be subject to copyright protection. No special steps have to be taken to obtain copyright. There are no application forms or registration certificates because copyright exists from the moment that the work in question comes into being.

The Copyright, Designs and Patents Act 1988 introduced major changes into copyright law. Under the Act, the basic principle is now that the first owner of literary, dramatic, musical or artistic works made by an employee in the course of his employment is his employer.

Occasionally, other legal provisions are relevant; for example, if you design toys or other products, it may be possible to register the design in accordance with the rules laid down in the Registered Designs Act 1949, although these were significantly amended by the 1988 Act.

It is not unusual for employers to include a specific clause in their service agreements on the subject of copyright; an example appears in the typical form of agreement set out in Appendix 1. Such provisions occasionally help to eliminate uncertainty; often, they will also seek to strengthen and extend the company's rights. As ever, you should make sure that you have read the contract wording carefully, and that you have understood its implications, before making up your mind whether it is acceptable.

5.3 Inventions and patents

Whether you are specifically involved in research and development or merely possess an inventive turn of mind, it is worth considering what is to happen if, while you are employed, you have an idea which can be commercially exploited.

Once again, the scope of your contractual duties is an important factor in assessing your legal position. If you make an invention connected with your work, the Patents Act 1977 provides that it will belong to your employer if:

1. made in the course of normal duties, when an invention might reasonably be expected to result; or
2. made in the course of duties specifically assigned to you, where it was reasonable to expect an invention to occur; or if
3. you had a special obligation to further the interests of your employer's business.

Any other invention belongs to you. You can, if you wish, assign it to your employer. If you do, he becomes the person to whom a patent may be granted.

You are entitled to compensation from your employer in respect of an invention which either originally belonged to him or which you assigned to him if:

(a) the invention was of outstanding benefit to him; or
(b) was transferred to him pursuant to an agreement which did not adequately benefit you.

Service agreements often require you to assign inventions and the patent rights in them to the company; a typical clause is included in Appendix 1. While any such stipulation needs to be carefully vetted, it is at least comforting to know that a contract which diminishes your rights in any invention or under a patent for it is unenforceable. Similarly, the Patents Act insists that an agreement by which you transfer a patent to your employer or give him an exclusive licence of it cannot prejudice your statutory right in compensation.

The way in which the law operates is shown by the case of *Reiss Engineering Co Ltd v Harris* (1985). Mr Harris was manager of a valve department. While working out his redundancy notice, he invented an improved form of valve and in due course he was granted a patent. The company claimed ownership of it.

A judge in the Patents Court decided that Mr Harris had not made his invention in the course of his normal duties. His primary duties were marketing and providing after-sales service; he was not employed to design and invent. Although he was one of the most highly paid men in the company, he did not attend board meetings or have the power to hire and fire. The judge thought that he was under no special obligation to further the business of Reiss, over and above his basic duties. Consequently the invention belonged to Mr Harris.

5.4 Trade secrets and confidential information

During the course of your job, you will probably learn a good deal about your employer's business methods. The information which comes into your possession will often be eagerly sought after by his competitors. It is not surprising that many companies impose stringent confidentiality obligations on their employees, either in the main body of a service agreement or in a separate letter that contains an undertaking to observe secrecy.

Even if nothing is put in writing, the law implies a number of limits on the extent to which you can make use of or disclose the knowledge derived from your work. That knowledge can be divided into three classes.

First, there are trade secrets. Even if you learn them by heart, you are not allowed to use them for the benefit of anyone but your employer.

Second, there is confidential information. The law will protect it on the basis that it was imparted to you in confidence or because it was obviously private, despite the fact that it becomes part of your own skill and expertise.

Third, there is general know-how. Typically, this is information of limited importance which is freely available elsewhere.

You can disclose information falling into the third class with impunity, either during or after your employment. There is nothing to stop you making use of such knowledge for your own personal benefit. Conversely, you are not allowed to reveal trade secrets at any time. Confidential information occupies a legal category between these two extremes. You should not disclose it while your job continues, but once it is over, you can do so unless you are bound by a specific, enforceable contractual duty not to.

So how can you tell the difference between a trade secret and confidential information? The need to make the distinction is most likely to arise when you leave and wish to know how far you can exploit your knowledge without falling foul of the law. There is further discussion on the practical implications of this in Chapter 21. However, it is as well to grasp from the beginning of your employment the classification into which the various parts of that knowledge fall. Unless you understand the thinking behind the jargon in the contract offered to you, you will not be able to make a reasoned decision about whether or not to sign it without quibbling.

Secrets come in many shapes and sizes, varying with the nature of the industry in which you work. They may range from the relatively unsophisticated, like the names and addresses of key customers and the prices that they are prepared to pay, to the highly complex, such as the chemical formulation of a newly developed product.

Unfortunately, there is no simple, concise legal test for drawing the line between data that is secret and data that is merely confidential. Useful guidance was, nevertheless, provided by the Court of Appeal in a case discussed further in Chapter 21. The Court of Appeal suggested that relevant factors in assessing the extent of your obligations include:

1. The nature of your job. Do you regularly handle secret information? If so, it may be taken that you are aware of its sensitivity.
2. The nature of the information itself. If it is only known to a few senior executives, it is more likely to be a trade secret.
3. The attitude of your employer. Does he emphasise to you the secrecy of the information?
4. Whether the data concerned can easily be isolated from other information passed to you. If it is part of a package which, as a whole, is non-secret, it is less likely to be regarded as a trade secret itself.

Check the wording of any secrecy undertaking that you are asked to sign. Clause 5 in Appendix 1 illustrates the kind of broad restriction that is frequently encountered. You and your employer may both benefit if an attempt is made to define in a rather more specific way the type of information that is to be kept secret after you leave.

5.5 Involvement in another business

The law demands that you act honestly towards your employer and work exclusively for him during the hours that you are contractually required to do so. Even outside working hours, you may be breaking your implied duty of good faith by 'moonlighting': setting up or involving yourself in a rival business. This might include merely preparatory acts, such as arranging for the formation of a limited company as a vehicle for your proposed activities.

As a broad rule of thumb, the more senior you are, and the greater access you have to your employer's trade secrets, the greater the onus will be upon you not to place yourself in a conflict of loyalties.

If you engage in some other work during your spare time which does not involve direct or indirect competition with your employer, it may not be fair to dismiss you unless you are contravening a specific restriction. For this reason many companies include in their standard contracts a clause requiring employees to devote their whole time and attention to the business and not to be involved in any other enterprise. Sometimes it is stated that this bar does not prevent you from taking a minority shareholding in a quoted company as a genuine investment. Clause 3(e) in Appendix 1 shows a conventional formula.

While the courts are sometimes hostile towards restraints upon what you do after the job ends, you will find it much more difficult to contest the validity of a clause that simply deals with what happens during your period of employment and that does not prevent you from earning your livelihood. If you do intend to pursue other interests during your own time, or wish at least to reserve the right to do so, the answer is to negotiate suitable contract terms.

For example, if your plans are clear – perhaps because you are continuing a long-established sideline – management may agree to exclude a list of activities from the scope of the prohibition. Another possibility is to insert a clause saying that spare-time working will be allowed if prior written permission is obtained and that such permission will not be unreasonably withheld.

5.6 Garden leave

'Garden leave' clauses are becoming fashionable in employment contracts. They are popular with employers but much less attractive from the point of view of a business executive.

In essence, a garden leave clause provides that the company is under no obligation to give the executive work to do. It may say specifically that the company has the right at any time to suspend the executive from performance of his duties or to exclude him from company premises, while providing that his right to receive his monthly pay cheque will be unaffected. In other words the company has the power to say to him: 'Go home and concentrate on digging your garden.'

If your contract contains a garden leave clause, the company is most likely to exercise its right under that clause if you resign or are given notice of termination. If your notice period is lengthy, then despite the continuing receipt of your remuneration, you may find life extremely frustrating. You would, for example, still be bound by your duty not to compete with the company while your employment continues during the notice period. What can you do?

The first point to make is that, if possible, you should resist the inclusion of a garden leave clause in your contract. It is a potentially unattractive and troublesome feature of the deal.

If you are unsuccessful in this, the Court of Appeal's decision in *Provident Financial Group plc and Whitegates Estate Agency Ltd v Hayward* (1989) offers some comfort. Mr Hayward was employed as financial director of an estate agency business under a contract which contained a garden leave clause. During his notice period, his employers decided that they did not want him to work out his notice. They were prepared to pay him in full for the balance of the period (nearly four months) provided that he did not work for anyone else and he thus began a period of garden leave. He wrote to the company announcing his intention to start work with a rival estate agency chain during his notice period and the company applied for an injunction preventing him from so doing.

The Court of Appeal decided that the judge in the High Court was right to refuse the company an injunction. The Court of Appeal judges were told that garden leave clauses were 'commonly included' in senior executives' service agreements and the judges themselves suggested that senior executives may 'hardly [be] in a position to negotiate over the terms of their contracts of service'. Both statements are perhaps questionable.

More convincing was the comment that: 'It is very common for employers to have somewhat exaggerated views of what will or may affect their businesses.' Lord Justice Dillon also acknowledged that an employee 'has a concern to work and a concern to exercise his skills'. That has been recognised in the past, in the case of some entertainers who depend on publicity, but Lord Justice Dillon thought it applied equally, 'to skilled workmen and even to chartered accountants'. There was no prospect of any serious or significant damage to the company's business from Mr Hayward working in his new job. His job was administrative and any confidential information which he had would not be relevant to a new employer.

Bear in mind, however, that you cannot be certain of a similar outcome in your own individual circumstances. Garden leave clauses are sometimes effective; an example is provided by the case of *Evening Standard Co Ltd v Henderson* (1987), which is discussed in Chapter 21.

5.7 Competition after you leave

No employer is entitled to compel you to enter into a contract which is designed simply, and without justification, to prevent you from competing in any way with his business once your job ends. Covenants in restraint of trade, as such prohibitions are called, are viewed with scepticism by the courts and are *prima facie* unenforceable.

That does not mean, though, that, after you leave, your former employer cannot prevent you from indulging in activities which damage his business, such as:

1. poaching your former colleagues;
2. poaching customers;
3. joining a rival organisation.

A covenant that restricts your freedom in one or more of these areas will be effective if your employer can show that it:

(a) is reasonable in the context of your employment relationship;
(b) is also reasonable when the public interest is taken into account;
(c) goes no further than is reasonably necessary for the protection of your employer's legitimate interests.

In the event of litigation at some future date, a judge will not look kindly upon a Draconian prohibition which might have the effect of depriving you of your ability to earn a living elsewhere. A bar on your involvement in a business which did not compete in any way with your former employer's enterprise would therefore seldom be upheld.

Well-advised companies take care not to be too ambitious when drafting restrictive covenants. For this reason, if you are a salesman, a restraint on poaching business may be limited to products with which you formerly dealt. Skilfully concocted clauses also often contain limits on your freedom to compete with your employer for a specific period of time after you go and within a particular area.

Generally speaking, the wider the area covered, the shorter the permissible time limit is likely to be and vice versa. In deciding whether or not a reasonable balance has been struck, it is also worth looking at factors such as:

- the nature of the business;
- your employer's scale of operations;
- your employment history and, especially, the extent of your personal contact with customers.

Thus, in *Greer v Sketchley Ltd* (1979), where an executive only worked in the Midlands and South East of England, albeit in a senior position, a covenant not to 'engage in any part of the UK in any business which is similar to any business . . . carried on by the Company' was too wide in area.

Nevertheless, the Court of Appeal added that if the company had operated all over England, Scotland and Wales, such a restriction might have been reasonable. This perhaps explains the different outcome in *Littlewoods Organisation Ltd v Harris* (1977) where a covenant extending nationwide survived judicial scrutiny. It was accepted that Littlewoods' reliance upon this clause was the only reasonable way to protect its national mail-order business when a key executive went to work with a direct competitor, taking with him confidential information about Littlewoods' catalogue and pricing structure.

In *Marley Tile Co Ltd v Johnson* (1982) the restriction was reasonable in terms of time limitation (one year) but not as regards the geographical area covered. It related to any area in which the employee had been employed at any time during the 12 months before the termination of his job. As Mr Johnson had changed location during that period, the covenant applied to almost the whole of Devon and Cornwall and the Court of Appeal considered that was too wide in his particular case.

A covenant against soliciting business was also ineffective because, on the evidence, there could have been 2500 customers in the counties in question. Mr Johnson would not have known more than a small percentage of them and, taking the size of the area, the number of customers and the type of products into account, the restraint was unreasonable.

Given the difficulty of predicting what a court may decide, many years hence, to be reasonable in the circumstances prevailing at that time, you should not be complacent when looking at the covenants to which your new employer wishes you to agree. To assume that a clause is too fierce to be enforced is risky. It might be safer to persuade your employer to modify it so that, while offering him some protection, it does not impinge too much upon your freedom of movement when your job ends. Coming up with a realistic restriction that represents a fair compromise will help you both to know where you stand.

Chapter 6

When Will Your Job End?

6.1 Looking ahead

From the time it is first offered to you, it makes sense to plan for the day when your job may end. This may sound like putting the cart before the horse and being unnecessarily pessimistic. The simple truth is, though, that you will never be in a better position to arrange suitable contract safeguards than during the period when a company is anxious to secure your services.

Failure to protect yourself adequately could prove costly. In later chapters, we shall look in more depth at the various job security rights that employees have gained through laws enacted in the past 25 years or so. But the fact remains that, for many business executives, the rights they have under their contract remain more valuable – certainly in hard cash terms.

You need, therefore, to anticipate both when your job might finish and how that might happen. Unless there are exceptional circumstances which render you liable to be sacked straight away (a few examples are set out in Clause 9 in the sample agreement in Appendix 1), you will be entitled to notice. The length of notice to which business executives are due varies greatly from company to company. Some otherwise generous companies offer even senior directors no more than three months' notice; at the other end of the scale, notice periods of three or even five years are by no means rare. Subject to limited minimum rights laid down by statute, which are explained below, there is often plenty of scope for negotiation. You should aim to strike a deal with your employers that gives you real peace of mind.

6.2 Retirement

Written contracts of employment sometimes do not deal with retirement. One reason is that there is often a well-established understanding that all jobs come to an end when their holders attain a certain age. The Sex Discrimination Act 1986 made it unlawful for an employer to discriminate between men and women as regards retirement age.

Nevertheless, it will eliminate the risk of misunderstanding if you and your employer discuss retirement specifically. During such talks, remember to look at any implications that the company's proposals may have for your pension.

A contractual agreement about retirement could also affect your statutory rights. For example, you cannot claim unfair dismissal if on or before the date when your job ends:

1. you have reached the normal retiring age for an employee holding the position which you held; or, if there is no normal retiring age,
2. you have reached the age of 65 (whether you are a man or woman).

When there is a contractual retiring age for all or nearly all employees in a particular job, that is presumed to be the normal retiring age. This presumption can be rebutted by evidence that there is in practice some higher age at which employees in that job are regularly retired and which they have reasonably come to regard as their normal retiring age.

In the context of unfair dismissal it is not your personal situation that is to be considered, but that of an employee in your category. If there is a normal retiring age for employees in your category, it cannot be displaced by an agreement to extend the retirement age in your own case. So if you are dismissed before the agreed age, you might have a claim for breach of contract, but not for unfair dismissal if you are over the normal retiring age for colleagues in your class of work.

6.3 Notice

Either your employer or yourself will normally be able to bring your job to an end by giving notice. As a business executive, your notice entitlement is an immensely significant part of your overall job rights. It is not legally necessary for the same notice entitlement to apply to both you and your employer. Ideally, you will be due a lengthy period of notice if your employer wishes you to leave. On the other hand, you will probably not wish to be subject to a correspondingly onerous commitment if you are the one who is keen to go. Saying this is, of course, much easier than persuading an employer to agree to it.

Minimum notice

Your minimum notice rights are laid down by the Consolidation Act, which in this respect covers almost all UK-based executives, although some classes of employee, including some part-timers, are excluded. The minimum notice period is geared to length of service:

Period of continuous employment	*Minimum notice*
At least four weeks and less than two years	One week
At least two years and less than twelve years	One week for each year of continuous employment
At least twelve years	Twelve weeks

The minimum notice that you must give your employer is one week, regardless of your length of service. You cannot 'contract out' of these rights. So if you enter into an agreement which provides for less than the statutory minimum notice, the above rules will still apply. You can, however, waive your right to notice should you wish to do so, and naturally you can agree with your employer to receive a payment in lieu of notice, if that suits you both.

Reasonable notice

If nothing is agreed about notice, the common law implies a term into the contract that it can be brought to an end if 'reasonable notice' is given. The problem is, what is reasonable in your particular case?

So much depends upon individual circumstances that little would be gained from cataloguing here the many court cases on this subject over the past century or so. Despite that, one can suggest a few guidelines.

Your seniority will often be a key factor, as will the degree of responsibility entrusted to you and, perhaps, your length of service.

A court might also take into account your salary level, skill and qualifications, together with, possibly, the difficulty that you would have in finding another suitable post. This last point could assume importance if, say, you were over the age of 50 or working in a field where the supply of skills exceeds demand.

Despite the disadvantages of uncertainty, you might be willing to leave the question of notice rights unresolved if you have strong grounds for suspecting that your employer would only agree to statutory minimum notice because that is company policy. This could leave you a little room to argue, should the need ever arise, that reasonable notice in your case was a longer period, such as six or 12 months. That kind of approach is, however, very much second best in comparison to a negotiated deal which provides you with genuine job security.

6.4 Fixed-term contracts

Fixed-term contracts are popular with many employers. They involve an agreement that the job will last for a specified period of time, although often provisions are included to enable the contract to be renewed if so desired. Although fixed terms allow for the job to end through a 'natural break', the expiry of a fixed period of employment still counts as a dismissal for some legal purposes, such as the right to claim unfair dismissal or redundancy pay.

Excluding statutory rights

Having said that, one notable attraction of fixed terms from an employer's point of view is that they offer a possible means of cutting out statutory rights, if a number of conditions are met. Thus:

1. a fixed-term contract for one year or more entered into from 1 October 1980 can include an agreement in writing by you to exclude any claim that you may have for unfair dismissal, where your dismissal consists only of the expiry of the term;
2. a fixed-term contract for two years or more entered into from 6 December 1965 can include an agreement in writing by you to exclude any claim that you may have for state redundancy pay, where your dismissal consists only of the expiry of the term.

Such exclusions need not be contained in the original contract document, but you must agree to them in writing before the term expires for them to be legally effective. In any event, they only relate to non-renewal of the contract when it runs out. They do not apply if your employment is terminated during the term or if you are constructively dismissed.

You may be presented with a service agreement which covers many pages and which, you are told, offers the attractive guarantee of a long working period. It goes without saying that you should study it with the utmost care. Towards the back, you may find exclusions of statutory rights which have never been mentioned in your discussions with management. Think before you sign. Is it really necesary for you to have no claim if you are indeed made redundant or treated unjustly at the time when the contract finishes? It is seldom unreasonable to ask for the exclusions to be deleted.

Directors' service agreements
The Companies Act 1985 provides that, if a company director's service agreement is to last for more than five years, it must be approved by the shareholders.

If this applies to you, make sure that the necessary resolution is passed before the agreement is signed. Failure to do so will mean that your efforts in negotiating long-term security of tenure might be in vain, as you could eventually find the sharcholders deciding to bring your contract to a premature end and discover that you are unable to claim compensation for the full period during which you expected to work.

Fixed-term or rolling contract?
When discussing terms with your employer, you may be asked to consider whether you prefer a fixed-term agreement or a 'rolling' contract, ie one which rolls on until the required period of notice is given.

There is no magic answer to this question. You simply have to weigh up your personal circumstances and what you are looking for from the job, keeping in mind any long-term plans that you may have for your future career development. Does it suit you to have a specific initial commitment, culminating in a natural break when you can leave and pursue other interests? Or would you rather have the security of knowing that, whenever in the years to come your employer may decide, for whatever reason, that you should go, you will be cushioned by a generous notice period which allows you to look for something else without the fear that very shortly the money will be running out? You are the best judge.

Chapter 7

Working Overseas

7.1 Special problems

The prospect of working overseas is attractive to many people. Before you accept a seemingly glamorous offer of a job abroad, however, it is important to pay careful attention to a number of legal and practical points.

In particular you need to face up to the reality that you are likely to have fewer employment rights than a colleague based in the UK. The rights that you do possess may be tricky to enforce. If difficulties do arise during your time abroad, you may feel isolated and vulnerable to pressure both from local management and head office.

Your aim should be to make sure that your agreed deal addresses the questions that are most likely to arise. But you have to be realistic. There is a big difference between the terms that you may be able to negotiate with, say, a US company seeking to recruit you to work in the Middle East and those offered by, say, a West German company offering a job at their headquarters, for which you are competing with a West German national. In the latter case, if you try to drive too hard a bargain, you may find that the offer is withdrawn.

7.2 Which legal system applies?

A well-drafted agreement will normally include a provision, known as a 'proper law' or 'governing law', which is along the following lines: 'This agreement shall be interpreted and enforced in accordance with the Laws of England.'

Normally, this stipulation is tucked away towards the end of the contract. The wording may look innocuous, but it is of vital importance. If your agreement is to be interpreted in accordance with English law, you will be able to take advice on its contents from your English lawyer. If the law of an overseas country applies, however, you would be wise to consult a lawyer familiar with the legal system of that country. The guidance given in this book applies to contracts governed by English law.

If the contract does not specify the 'proper law', tricky questions can arise. The basic principle under English law is that the law which the parties intend to apply will govern the agreement. In assessing that intention, the courts will take into account the connection that the contract and the parties have with a particular country.

Even so, the mere fact that an employee is English, his contract is written in English and his salary is payable in pounds sterling will not always be decisive. These factors were present in the agreement considered in the case of *Sayers v International Drilling Co NV* (1971). However, the employer was a Dutch company which used the same form of contract to employ Europeans of various nationalities for work outside the UK. The court decided that Dutch law applied.

The only safe course, therefore, is to make sure that the contract clearly states which legal regime applies to your employment.

7.3 Do you lose your statutory rights?

A majority of overseas workers are disqualified from the employment protection rights laid down in UK legislation. The precise formula for working out who is eligible depends upon the legal entitlement in question. The most important is the right not to be unfairly dismissed, from which employees who ordinarily work outside Great Britain are excluded.

But what does 'ordinarily' mean? The difficulties of interpreting the law are shown by a number of cases that have arisen.

In *Wilson v Maynard Ship Building Consultants AB* (1977) a staff consultant was employed by a Swedish company from July 1973 until his dismissal in September 1975. He had a written employment contract, but it did not refer to his place of work. It had been agreed that in effect he was to work as required in any country in which his employers had contracts. The evidence was that he had worked in the UK for 40 weeks and in Italy for 50 weeks. The Court of Appeal rejected the view that had previously held sway, namely that it was possible for any employee to work both ordinarily in Great Britain and outside it. It must, said the judges, be one or the other.

A number of principles for ascertaining where an employee 'ordinarily' works were suggested. First, you should examine what the terms of your contract require rather than what actually happened during the existence of that contract. Suppose, for example, you are employed for three years, of which the first is to be spent abroad and the other two in Great Britain. If you are dismissed at the end of your first year, concentrating on the terms of the contract leads to the conclusion that you ordinarily worked in Great Britain, whereas looking at what actually happened leads to the opposite conclusion.

Second, if your employer has discretion as to where you should work, the usual approach in law is to ask what your base is, as indicated by the contract terms. In the absence of special factors, the base is likely to be the place where you ordinarily work, even though in fact you spend more time away from your base than you do there.

Finally, in determining your base, all relevant contractual terms should be examined. These might include terms defining your headquarters, indicating where travel involved in your job begins and ends, where and in what currency you are to be paid and whether or not you are obliged to pay UK National Insurance contributions.

These general principles were subsequently considered in *Todd v British Midland Airways Ltd* (1978). The employee was an airline pilot employed by a company established in Great Britain, but he spent just over half his flying days outside Great Britain. Following the approach suggested in the Wilson case, the Court of Appeal held that the pilot was eligible for unfair dismissal rights. However, it was said that looking at the employee's base was not the be-all and end-all. The base was merely one of the factors which should normally be considered. Lord Denning expressed the view that, in any event, in ascertaining where the base was, the contract terms were often of little help and 'you have to go by the conduct of the parties and the way they have been operating the contract'.

A third Court of Appeal decision, *Janata Bank v Ahmed* (1981), has also suggested that the question of one's base should not assume overriding importance. Mr Ahmed commenced work in Bangladesh in 1972. He was soon posted to England and then for a short period to Brussels before leaving the Bank in 1975. The Court of Appeal concluded that he ordinarily worked outside Great Britain and was therefore unable to pursue an unfair dismissal claim. Despite the fact that he had worked for most of the period of his contract in England, lived in England, was paid in English currency and paid National Insurance contributions in the UK, he was at all times liable to be recalled to Dhaka.

Nevertheless, it is still useful to ask what your base is. And even if you lose your statutory job rights for a period while working abroad, you may regain them if you return to work in this country. This possibility arises from the complex statutory definition of your period of 'continuous employment'. Almost certainly, you will benefit from taking expert professional advice on the extent of your statutory rights, should you wish to attempt to take advantage of them.

7.4 Protecting your position

If you are planning to work overseas for an organisation with which you are not very familiar, it makes sense to check that they are a *bona fide*, reputable organisation with a good track record of treating executive employees fairly.

Even if that is confirmed, it is often unwise not to seek additional safeguards in your contract. The kind of protection that you may require depends to some extent on the status of your employer. There are three main possibilities:

1. you may be employed by a UK company to work abroad;
2. you may work for an overseas subsidiary of a UK company;
3. your employer may be based principally or wholly overseas.

Parent company guarantees

Joining an overseas subsidiary, for example, carries potential risks. The business might one day be sold off, wound up or nationalised by the host government. The danger is that your rights of legal redress in such cases will be limited or non-existent in practice. When your job ends, you may have to return to the UK. Even if the subsidiary is still in existence, you will find that conducting litigation from a distance is extremely troublesome, however viable your claim appears to be on paper.

With this in mind, it is often worth seeking some form of guarantee from the parent company. Naturally, some parent companies are reluctant to give sweeping guarantees, but the arguments in favour of them are strong from the expatriate's point of view, especially if he is being asked to transfer from the parent to a less substantial overseas subsidiary. If a guarantee is to be given, the best approach is for the parent company to become a party to your contract and it is desirable for the document to be under seal.

Naturally, the form of guarantee that is appropriate varies from case to case. A typical formula provides that the parent company will indemnify an expatriate against any loss or expense he may suffer as a result of a breach of contract by the subsidiary, for instance if the employment is terminated before the expiry of a specified fixed term. The guarantee should provide the expatriate with a direct claim against the parent which is enforceable in the most convenient (usually English) courts. Again, it is essential to seek legal advice on the precise wording to be used.

Repatriation provisions
Clearly, you may face serious difficulties if your employment overseas is brought to an end before the anticipated date. The tax consequences, for instance, may prove disastrous. Ideally, your contract will provide that you will be guaranteed receipt of the same sum net of UK tax if you unexpectedly have to pay that tax. Realistically, however, only a limited number of employers are likely to agree to a potentially costly and open-ended liability of that sort.

Less ambitiously, you might ask your employer to agree to repatriate you, together with your family and possessions, free of charge, if your job ends prematurely for any reason, except perhaps if you have been dismissed for misconduct.

A problem arises with some deals of this kind. If your employment ends because of, say, revolution overseas, the contract may be regarded as frustrated, ie completely brought to an end by operation of law, because it is no longer possible for the contractual duties to be performed as you and your employer originally envisaged. In that event, an obligation to repatriate could be legally nullified. One imaginative solution is for a UK-based parent or associate of the overseas employer to guarantee repatriation as a separate and binding legal obligation.

7.5 Miscellaneous provisions

A wide range of other matters needs to be considered. While it is not possible to provide an exhaustive check-list, the following matters are especially relevant.

Salary, taxation etc
Your contract should clearly state the currency in which your salary is to be calculated and also the currency and place of pay. You will need to consider whether the suggested currency is strong enough in the context of anticipated fluctuations in the exchange rate. You must also take into account any local exchange control regulations,

the effect of which may make it sensible for the contract to stipulate that part of your salary shall be credited to you elsewhere.

You need to check on the tax position. A major attraction of working overseas may be the chance to escape from UK income tax. To achieve this, you have to serve a qualifying period overseas. Does the agreement cover this adequately? You should also bear in mind that social security payments might be higher abroad. If so, will your employer reimburse you?

Relocation
If you have to sell your present home, it is worth asking for your relocation costs, including estate agency fees and legal expenses, to be borne by your employer. Some employers insist that if an employee leaves the job for any reason within a specified time limit after moving overseas, all or part of the relocation expenses must be repaid. You need to give careful thought to any such stipulation before accepting it.

Your travel expenses, and those of your spouse and children if appropriate, should normally be borne by your employer. If you are to live in rented accommodation or a hotel while finding somewhere more permanent to live in your new domicile, your employer may be willing to be responsible for those costs. Complete reimbursement is obviously more attractive than a contribution of a fixed amount.

Ongoing expenses
You are likely to incur a variety of additional expenses by virtue of your move overseas. You may therefore wish your employer to agree to pay some or all of the following:

1. travel home at agreed intervals for yourself, your spouse and your children;
2. additional school fees if your children have to remain in the UK;
3. costs of medical and dental treatment overseas;
4. costs of air-conditioning and other utilities in your accommodation;
5. language tuition, if necessary.

What is appropriate will, naturally, vary from job to job and from country to country. Your overall objective should be to ensure that a deal that at first sight looks attractive is not, in the long run, undermined because you have to expend significant additional sums in order to maintain a reasonable life-style abroad and fulfil your duties adequately.

Chapter 8

Coping with Change

8.1 The need for flexibility

So much is at stake when you start a job that you owe it to yourself to think all the implications through. Is the deal right? Has it been accurately recorded? The easy option, of course, is to sign whatever 'company standard' agreement is put before you. It takes nerve to haggle over the small print if you are told that your new colleagues have worked under similar terms for years without batting an eyelid. Even so, at the very least you ought to make sure that you understand fully what you are committing yourself to before deciding whether you can afford not to press for the document to be amended.

Try gazing into your crystal ball. What problems might arise in the future? The preceding chapters have outlined many of the likely areas of difficulty. Once you have identified the points that are going to be crucial in your particular job, you may have to be persuasive if you want improved safeguards built into your agreement.

How successful you are in sorting matters out to your satisfaction will depend partly on your bargaining strength. Naturally, the company's resources will be greater than yours. Merely by having a contract designed to protect the interests of the business already prepared, your employer may seize the initiative in any negotiations. But if you can offer talents that are in short supply, you may be better able to extract concessions than you suppose.

Once suitable terms have been settled and, one hopes, clearly and concisely set out in a signed agreement, you will be in a position to give the job your undivided attention, secure in the knowledge that you have created the right conditions for job survival. Above all, it is a fundamenal principle of English law that a contract cannot be varied unilaterally. Consent to change is required.

It would be a mistake, though, to be complacent once the deal has finally been done. You still need to be prepared to cope with crises arising in the years to come. Industry does not stand still and the trend nowadays is for employers to expect their employees to respond positively to the demands of the enterprise. If you are intransigent, or are determined to stick to the letter of your contract come what may, you could be in for a rude awakening.

The reality is that having a comprehensive and fairly-balanced service agreement is a tremendous advantage to any executive, but it is not in itself enough. Ultimately, your personal qualities are most important. If job security is what you seek, then besides setting your agreement down in black and white, you should strive to be well organised, willing to discuss your grievances rather than bottling them up and prepared to react flexibly if circumstances change.

8.2 Keeping a job file

Your employer will have a personnel file containing a potted history of your career with the company. Why not do likewise and build up your own record of your progress within the organisation?

What goes into that file is up to you. It is useful to start with a copy of the advertisement which originally caught your eye, for the reasons mentioned in Chapter 1. Your application, CV, letter of appointment and job description all deserve to be kept, as well as any document containing contract terms or rules and procedures which affect you directly or indirectly.

For later reference, preserve any written job appraisal forms. It is even a good idea to hold on to congratulatory memos (perhaps appended to slips telling you of pay increases) or any other correspondence which might at some distant date help you to defend yourself against unfair criticisms of your capabilities.

It might also be prudent to make notes of any conversations which have a major bearing on your status or prospects and retain them in your job file. Even if you just use them as memory joggers, they could prove invaluable if there is ever a quarrel about who actually said what and when. Constructive dismissal cases (examined in Chapter 15) provide a good example of situations in which it is vital to have evidence of conduct on your employer's part which you find objectionable. Executives who can produce a reliable 'diary of events' to a court or tribunal often fare better than those who cannot. But do not go too far. Some executives think it is a good idea to make secret tape recordings of sensitive discussions with managers whom they are reluctant to trust. Occasionally – leaving any ethical questions aside – taped evidence can help to settle a point in dispute. On the whole, though, the cases in which covert taping of conversations plays a decisive part are few. Taping – secret or not – is very much a last resort.

8.3 Talking about problems

There is plenty of truth in the cliché that a trouble shared is a trouble halved. It may help to get an apparently overwhelming worry into perspective if you feel that you can talk about it to your superiors. The thinking behind the requirement that a statutory statement of terms should include a note dealing with the in-house grievance procedure is that many hiccups in the working relationship are best cured through level-headed discussion.

If you fall foul of your immediate superior for some reason, you may find that if you raise the matter with his boss, the problem can be resolved. In a well-run company there will be no question of simply rubber-stamping management decisions when a grievance or appeal is pursued.

All the same, it would be naive not to recognize that there are cases where executives are not going to achieve much without the assistance of detached yet sympathetic support from someone based outside the organisation. If the problem is serious or you feel you cannot be confident of an impartial assessment of your complaint from the key men in the corporate hierarchy, you will probably need to turn elsewhere.

Advice is available from many quarters. A solicitor well versed in employment law or a freelance personnel expert may be able to help, although you will be charged for their services and you need to be sure that they have a feet-on-the-ground approach in addition to technical competence.

There is an increasing tendency for cautious executives to obtain legal expenses insurance so that cost will not prove an obstacle if they ever need to call upon professional help. There are a number of good policies on the market nowadays and several insurance companies offer a hot-line consultancy service by way of practical support. But taking out your own cover may not be necessary if you belong to a trade association which offers its members the benefit of confidential advice if they run into difficulties at work. You may also be able to exchange ideas with fellow members who have, perhaps, encountered similar problems in the past.

Making use of government-funded resources may be worth considering. The Advisory, Conciliation and Arbitration Service (ACAS) offers practical assistance and you may find that a telephone call is enough to set your mind at rest. Although a branch of the Civil Service, ACAS aims for a pragmatic, not bureaucratic approach, and a number of ACAS officers have spent time working in industry.

If you think that you have suffered as a result of sex or race discrimination, the Equal Opportunities Commission and the Commission for Racial Equality are in a position not only to advise but also, if appropriate, to give financial backing if there is no viable alternative to mounting a legal challenge to your employer's behaviour.

8.4 Changes within the scope of your contract

No deal lasts for ever and not even the most skilful draftsman can cater for every eventuality when drawing up a service contract. If you are at some stage asked to undertake tasks with which you are unfamiliar, your starting point should be to ascertain whether you are, impliedly, obliged to do what is wanted.

For example, the question could be prompted by the introduction of new technology. The computer revolution may have a significant effect upon the way in which you are able to perform your job. The courts do not encourage Luddism. Inland Revenue employees discovered this when they took a claim – that the Revenue's requirement that they transfer from manual methods to using a computerised system was in breach of contract – to the High Court. Although the content of some of the jobs in question had altered considerably, the degree of that alteration was not sufficient to fall outside the original description of the proper function of the grade concerned.

The judgment in this case, *Cresswell and others v Board of Inland Revenue* (1984), contained robust comment on the need to move with the times:

> There really can be no doubt as to the fact than an exployee is expected to adapt himself to new methods and techniques introduced in the course of his employment . . . Of course in a proper case the employer must provide any necessary training . . . It will, in all cases, be a question of pure fact as to whether the re-training involves the acquisition of such esoteric skills that it would not be reasonable to expect the employee to acquire them . . . It can

hardly be considered that to ask an employee to acquire basic skills as to retrieving information from a computer . . . is something in the slightest esoteric or even, nowadays, unusual.

8.5 Refusing to change

If your employer's requirements do involve a change in the terms of your employment contract, you should think carefully before declining to agree. Although you cannot be forced to accept a variation in the agreement, your job may be at risk if you stand on your rights. This is because it is possible to dismiss fairly for a refusal to accept change.

The case of *R S Components Ltd v Irwin* (1974) affords a classic example of how that may occur. The company manufactured electrical components and suffered serious competition from ex-employees who set up in business themselves and poached the company's customers. Profits declined and salesmen's commission dropped. The company therefore said that salesmen must agree to a new restrictive covenant which barred them from soliciting customers for up to a year after leaving. Mr Irwin and three of his colleagues would not agree and were sacked.

Their unfair dismissal claims failed. The Employment Appeal Tribunal considered that there was a potentially fair reason for the dismissals and that the employer had in fact handled the matter fairly, adding:

> . . . it is not difficult to imagine a case where it would be essential for employers embarking for example on a new technical process to invite existing employees to agree to some reasonable restriction on their use of the knowledge they acquire of the new technique; and where it would be essential for the employer to terminate, by due notice, the services of an employee who was unwilling to accept such a restriction.

Thus it is clear that if the change is a realistic one and the company is justifiably convinced that it must be imposed, you will be extremely vulnerable if you do not fall in line. As a result, you may have little practical alternative but to agree to increased working hours or to work in a different area, despite the fact that the contract does not provide for such things, if they are commercially necessary from the point of view of the business.

Indeed, there have been decisions in which management's right to reorganise in a way contrary to the explicit terms of employee's contracts has been interpreted even more liberally. This was so in *Hollister v National Farmers' Union* (1979). The Union reorganised at the request of, and for the benefit of, its employees. Nevertheless, Mr Hollister resisted because, although his remuneration was improved, his previous rights were reduced. He was therefore sacked. The Court of Appeal held that his dismissal was fair and that it was not vitiated by a failure to consult him over the reorganisation. Even if a failure to implement the reorganisation would not bring the business to a standstill, dismissal for a failure to conform with it might be fair if there was 'some sound, good business reason for the reorganisation'. Such a principle can apply equally to a constructive dismissal; see Chapter 15.

Fortunately, tribunals do not altogether ignore the interests of the affected employee when adjudicating upon the fairness or otherwise of a company's actions. Whether or not the advantages to the business of imposing a change outweigh the disadvantages to the employee is one of the factors which should be taken into account. It seems, though, that even if you are being reasonable in refusing to agree to a change, that does not necessarily mean that it is unfair to push the change through and dismiss you because of your reluctance to go along with it. A tribunal will look at all the relevant facts before making up its mind. So you need to be well aware of the possible implications of continued resistance.

8.6 A change of employer

The arrival of new management can create tensions within any work-force. Chapter 9 looks at the familiar problem of personality clashes. Even more serious may be the effect of a take-over of the business that you work for. We saw in Chapter 3 that the law now offers you some protection if there is a 'transfer of undertaking', although not if there is a mere sale of shareholding control. Instead of being made redundant when the ownership of your employer changes hands, you are nowadays automatically transferred to work for the purchaser.

Nevertheless, you may still lose your job because of the take-over or for a reason connected with it. If so, whether you work for the buyer or the seller, you will be able to complain of unfair dismissal, subject to the normal eligibility rule outlined in Chapter 20.

If the only or main reason for your being sacked was an 'economic, technical or organisational' one, entailing changes in the work-force – the vague Euro-jargon of the 1981 Regulations is a reminder that they were inspired by an EC Directive – your claim will not succeed if you have been treated in a reasonable manner. Otherwise, the dismissal will, under special rules, be regarded as automatically unfair. Suffice it to say that such is the complexity of this area of the law that one case on the subject, discussed in Chapter 13, has already reached the House of Lords; it is unlikely to be the last.

Chapter 9

Personality Clashes and Discrimination

9.1 Conflicts at work

Unless you are very easy-going and also fortunate, you are bound sooner or later to meet someone through your job whom you find it impossible to like. Normally, you will be able to agree to disagree when necessary, but if conflicting attitudes spill over into lasting antagonism, then you are heading for trouble.

You should bend over backwards to avoid bitter personal rows and the holding of grudges. Whether your clash is with a colleague, superior or customer, allowing it to develop into a trial of strength could in the end seriously jeopardise your career.

Sometimes, alas, you will have little control over the matter. In particular, you may gain the impression that you are being victimised because of what you are, rather than because of who you are. Even in these supposedly progressive times, you might be passed over for promotion or unkindly treated because of your sex or racial origins. If that happens, you may wish to exercise the rights that Parliament has granted to victims of discrimination to make a complaint to an industrial tribunal.

There is often much to be said for trying to sort the matter out by pursuing your rights under your company's grievance procedure. If it is possible to put your point of view frankly to an impartial and sympathetic individual, it may be that the difficulties that have arisen can be resolved without the need for drastic action on anyone's part.

9.2 Incompatible individuals

Fellow employees

If you fall out with someone in your own office or factory, the working atmosphere may become intolerable, not just for the two of you, but also for your colleagues.

You should not let a rift with a subordinate widen to such an extent; to do so will probably call your managerial qualities into question. Conversely, if you have a serious disagreement with your boss, it could so adversely affect your standing in the firm that you may decide you would be better off elsewhere.

If your superiors get wind that you are feuding with a fellow employee, they may intervene in the hope of sorting the problem out. Obviously, it is sensible to co-operate with them. The ultimate sanction may be for them to sack the person whom they regard as being mainly to blame. For this to be fair, they should investigate the conflict in depth, trying to persuade the parties to bury the hatchet and work constructively together. In short, a mere breakdown in a working relationship does not in itself justify dismissal unless, after a reasonable attempt to effect a reconciliation, it is found to be beyond remedy.

Outsiders
It would be galling to lose your job because of a dispute with a customer or client, when your employer regards you as a capable performer, but this can occur if somehow you offend a person or organisation whose business is valuable to your company.

Again, a fair employer should look thoroughly into the background and, by way of discussion, try to achieve an amicable solution. Yet if the customer is adamant that you must go and you cannot be fitted into another niche where you would have no contact with him, you may be vulnerable to dismissal.

For action of this kind to be fair, the risk that you may suffer an injustice should be considered before a final decision is taken. So said the Court of Appeal in *Dobie v Burns International Security Services (UK) Ltd* (1984), a case in which the employer's services were governed by a contract with a local authority that gave the council the right 'to approve or otherwise the employment or continued employment of any member of the company'. Mr Dobie was dismissed at the behest of an agent of the council. The Court of Appeal indicated that, in circumstances like these, factors to be taken into account include:

1. your length of service;
2. whether your job performance and attitude have been satisfactory over the years;

3. the difficulties that you may encounter in obtaining alternative employment.

9.3 Sexual harassment

Until a few years ago, the existence of sexual harassment as a genuine problem in many businesses was scarcely acknowledged. In 1977, though, Lord Justice Lawton included in a list of examples of conduct that could amount to constructive dismissal 'persistent and unwanted amorous advances by an employer to a female employee'.

One bizarre early case that reached the law reports concerned the lesbian harassment of a young woman by her employer's wife. More recently, there has been a flood of more conventional sexual harassment claims brought by women, including women occupying executive roles in large companies; this is by no means exclusively a problem of women on the factory floor or in the typing pool who have reacted adversely to what their male colleagues and superiors may have tried to excuse as 'a bit of harmless fun'.

No one has yet formulated an entirely comprehensive definition of sexual harassment, but the key components of such conduct are that it is sexual in nature and unwanted. A victim (and in theory he could be male, although no man has yet, apparently, pursued a sexual harassment claim through the courts) can leave and complain of unfair constructive dismissal but will often prefer to keep the option of staying on in the job and bringing a sex discrimination claim instead. Furthermore, a claim of discrimination can be brought by someone who lacks the necessary qualifying service for unfair dismissal rights.

Such an action succeeded in *Strathclyde Regional Council v Porcelli* (1986). A female employee was offensively treated by two male colleagues, but at first her claim was rejected because the industrial tribunal felt that, had she been a man, she would still have been harassed, although the specific nature of the unpleasantness might have been different. Rejecting that conclusion, the Scottish Court of Session said that if the unfavourable treatment included a significant sexual element to which a person of the opposite sex would not have been vulnerable, that amounted to discrimination.

9.4 Sex and race discrimination

More than a decade after the introduction of legislation against sex or race discrimination, it remains true that only a minority of senior business executives are women or members of racial minority groups. There are no doubt many reasons for this; one of them is that unspoken, perhaps sometimes subconscious, prejudice remains deeply ingrained in many management structures.

Despite that, surprisingly few complaints about discrimination are made to industrial tribunals each year. Even fewer succeed and the average level of compensation in those cases is just a few hundred pounds. Small wonder, perhaps, that claims are seldom made by people who enjoy executive status. Nevertheless, the topic is undeniably an important one and it is worth sketching in the legal rules.

Discrimination on the basis of sex or race may be direct or indirect. You are directly discriminated against if treated less favourably than a person of the opposite sex is or would be treated, or if you are treated less favourably on racial grounds.

Indirect sex discrimination occurs where you have to comply with a requirement which is, or would be, applied equally to a person of the opposite sex, but:

1. which is such that the proportion of members of your sex who can comply is considerably smaller than the corresponding proportion of members of the opposite sex;
2. which is to your detriment because you cannot comply with it; and
3. which cannot be shown to be justifiable irrespective of the person to whom it is applied.

Similarly, indirect race discrimination occurs when a person applies a requirement which he applies or would apply to persons of a different racial group but:

(a) which is such that the proportion of people of the victim's racial group who can comply is considerably smaller than the proportion of the people not of that group who can comply;
(b) which is to the detriment of the victim because he or she cannot comply with it; and
(c) which cannot be shown to be justifiable irrespective of the colour, race, nationality or ethnic origins of the person to whom it is applied.

The statutory framework is supported by Codes of Practice issued by the Equal Opportunities Commission and the Commission for Racial Equality. If you feel that you have been discriminated against, it may be a good idea to contact whichever of those two bodies is appropriate for further guidance.

Chapter 10

Criticisms of Your Job Performance

10.1 Is anything wrong?

Judging one's own strengths and weaknesses is far from easy. However self-critical you may be – and some executives set themselves standards of achievement which are unrealistically high, rather than too low – there is usually much to be gained from learning the views of others about your capabilities. Listening to a balanced, impartial opinion, even if it contains an element of constructive criticism of certain aspects of your work, should help you to make the most of your potential.

Many companies operate regular job appraisals, often on an annual basis. An endless variety of approaches is adopted. Assessment methods range from the formal and sophisticated to the haphazard. Large organisations with substantial personnel management resources tend to grade employees each year, arranging in-depth discussions and permitting appeals against adverse markings. They see this as a way of helping to ensure that their employees do not get a raw deal – for example, when candidates for promotion are being compared.

You may be encouraged to formulate a job plan which goes beyond the scope of your basic job description, itemising a series of personal objectives for the year ahead. This is often a useful exercise, although there is occasionally a risk that the emphasis upon paperwork becomes so great that everyone loses sight of what was originally intended. It is best to concentrate upon essentials and for forms to be used mainly as *aides-mémoire*.

In smaller businesses, job reviews may only take place when the time comes to decide on salary increases and there might be little consultation with the majority of members of staff. An extreme example of hit-or-miss judgment on performance occurred in *Payne v Spook Erection Ltd* (1984) where a company established a weekly 'merit table' in which workers were assessed largely by guesswork. A foreman who became disenchanted with this system and reluctant to apply it was fired; predictably, his unfair dismissal claim succeeded.

An effective method of appraisal will benefit both you and the business. It gives everyone an opportunity to take stock. If you can be confident that the person in charge is both perceptive and fair, the review meeting should be something to welcome, not to dread. You have nothing to gain from staying in the dark about what your superiors really think of your job performance. On the contrary, a company that does not keep an eye on how its employees are functioning is probably itself being badly run.

A worthwhile appraisal will involve more than a mere pronouncement on the quality of your recent work, a pat on the head or a kick on the backside as the case may be. There ought to be scope for feedback, a chance for you to express whatever thoughts or concerns you may have at the time. Dialogue, not a monologue, is called for.

You should, of course, be judged in relation to what you are employed, and reasonably expected, to do, not by any other touchstone. So, to take one illustration from the law reports, if you are the company's assistant accountant, it could be unfair to dismiss you for alleged lack of management ability if that has no real bearing on your daily tasks. You need to know what is required of you. Once again, the desirability of clear terms of contract, coupled perhaps with an unambiguous job description, is plain.

Complaints

Any significant criticisms made of you deserve careful attention. You may, for example, have a powerful defence to a vague statement that your work leaves something to be desired. What evidence is there that you are not living up to the appropriate standards?

Of course, the quality of an executive is not always easily defined. But a mere 'gut feeling' on the part of your superiors that you fall short of what is expected, when they cannot put their fingers on what is wrong, is not really good enough.

Executives sometimes find that, on close inspection, the complaints made against them are misconceived. In a simple case, a salesman's failure to achieve normal and apparently realistic targets might be due to a change in the size or nature of his territory or other factors which are entirely beyond his personal control. A finance director challenged about the emergence of unexpected cash flow problems may be able to point out that they are due to invoicing delays caused by the breakdown of a new computer system, purchased and installed without sufficient thought and against his advice.

Difficulties may arise if your company has recently undergone a change in top management, perhaps following a take-over of the business. If, after a previously unblemished career, you are taken to task, it may be that your superiors' requirements are unrealistic or that you have not yet been given sufficient time to adjust to the style of the new regime.

Another possibility is that you may be treated inconsistently. It may be extremely hard for your employer to justify a poor grading at assessment time when earlier in the year you received a letter from the chairman specifically thanking and praising you for your efforts. You may also be able to refer back to a recent rise in merit pay or bonus in your response. Baffling contradictions in the attitude of management happen more often that one might imagine. When they occur, you will be glad that you kept a record of your continuing achievements in your job file.

Even when there is a grain or more of truth in a criticism, you may not be wholly or, indeed, mainly to blame. In order to give of your best, you need:

1. adequate training in up-to-date working practices;
2. wholehearted co-operation from your colleagues;
3. consistent support from your superiors.

If one or more of these features is missing from your working life, you should make it known and strive to ensure that management is committed to improving matters.

10.2 Opportunities to improve

Employees who perform poorly can be fairly dismissed. An employer should not, however, react excessively or too soon if you make a mistake. Giving you a fair deal means that he should follow a reasonable procedure before taking a final decision that you must part company. This means that, having discussed the problems with you, he should make you aware of the consequences of a continuing failure to live up to expectations and give you an opportunity to demonstrate an improvement. While what he says may not add up to a warning in the strict disciplinary sense, you should be left in no doubt about where you stand.

Criticisms of Your Job Performance

It is impossible to lay down hard and fast rules as to what constitutes a realistic improvement period. No case is likely to be identical in all respects with another. Relevant factors will include:

1. the nature of your job;
2. your length of service;
3. your seniority;
4. your past record.

Useful guidance of a general nature can be found in the ACAS handbook *Discipline at Work*, and the law reports provide numerous examples of the way in which the courts and tribunals have dealt with specific cases. About 15 years ago, three months was considered to be sufficient time for a sales director with two years' service to convince his company of his competence. Yet not too long afterwards, it was suggested that for a salesman with 20 years' continuous employment, three years was an appropriate improvement period; many would think that to be erring on the high side. Whatever length of time is given, though, it will be difficult for an employer to justify dismissing you on the grounds of lack of skills or basic ability within that time unless something exceptional happens.

One curious issue is the different view taken by different courts of the significance of an employee's seniority. One judge has said that:

> those employed in senior management may by the nature of their jobs be fully aware of what is required of them and fully capable of judging for themselves whether they are achieving that requirement. In such circumstances the need for warning and an opportunity to improve are much less apparent.

This contrasts with the statement in another case that:

> when you have a man . . . in a managerial capacity, there is a greater obligation on the employer to take preliminary steps to bring to the manager's notice that he, the employer, is contemplating a possible dismissal.

There is unanimity, though, that normally you must understand that your job is in jeopardy and have the chance to improve your standards before it will be fair to sack you.

10.3 Special problems

Gross negligence

If your inadequacy is so serious that, to use one phrase from the case law, there is an 'irredeemable incapability', so that being given a warning and an opportunity to mend your ways would simply be a waste of time and might put the business at risk, it may be just to dismiss you as soon as the full extent of your failings comes to light.

In practice, this principle should not often be relevant in the case of experienced executives. If you were so evidently inept, why did the company see fit to give you the job in the first place?

Disastrous errors

There are some high-risk jobs in which an employer dare not continue to employ a person who makes a mistake because the effect of a repetition could be horrific.

In this connection, it has been pointed out that:

> The passenger-carrying airline pilot, the scientist operating the nuclear reactor, the chemist in charge of research into the possible effects of, for example, Thalidomide, the driver of the Manchester to London express, the driver of an articulated lorry full of sulphuric acid, are all in a position in which one failure to maintain the proper standard of professional skill can bring about a major disaster.

The illustrations can, of course, be multiplied, but it is important to bear in mind that such cases are exceptional. Most errors have much less dramatic consequences.

Intransigence

An employer complaining about your performance ought to behave reasonably. Similarly, you should react in a sensible manner. If you feel upset by an apparent unfairness, pursue the matter through the grievance procedure. At all costs avoid adopting a pig-headed attitude.

If you are unnecessarily intransigent, you may be jeopardising your career. Lord Denning is among those who have emphasised that fair play may not always require that you be given a warning and time to improve if you refuse to acknowledge blatant fault on your part:

> In some cases, it may be proper and reasonable to dismiss at once, especially with a man who is determined to go his own way.

Foolish pride can carry a high price tag.

Over-promotion

Laurence J Peter's famous Principle states that:

> In a hierarchy every employee tends to rise to his level of incompetence ... in time every post tends to be occupied by an employee who is incompetent to carry out its duties.

While that may be an exaggeration, there is no doubt that some promotions do fail to work out, even where there is no shortage of training, supervision and support. If you are unfortunate enough not to make the grade in a new and elevated position, you do not have an automatic right to return to your old job, although in a minority of cases you may be able to negotiate an agreement that this should happen.

You should, of course, still be treated fairly and this may entail your employer looking round his organisation, perhaps even the whole corporate group of which he is part, to see if you can be fitted in elsewhere at an appropriate level, before finally deciding to terminate your employment. You may well, in the circumstances, be willing to take a step backwards rather than lose your job.

10.4 Can you be sued?

If a mistake on your part costs your employer money, could he seek to recover his losses by taking you to court?

The Court of Appeal made it clear in *Janata Bank v Ahmed* (1981) that this is certainly a possibility. Even if nothing is said specifically, there is an implied term in your employment contract that you owe a duty to exercise reasonable care and skill in carrying out your job. A High Court judgment ordering Mr Ahmed, a former assistant general manager of a bank, to compensate his former employers to the tune of more than £30,000 in respect of losses caused by his negligence, was therefore upheld.

Before you have too many sleepless nights, it is worth noting Lord Justice Ackner's comment that, in practice, employers are more likely to use the sanction of dismissal than a High Court writ. He added:

> There is after all no point in throwing good money after bad, and the need to maintain harmonious industrial relations is likely to be considered of greater importance than achieving a barren judgment.

Chapter 11

Sickness and Absence From Work

11.1 The risks

Many employers keep a close eye on absence levels. If you are away from work for a lengthy period, or for short spells at frequent intervals, your job may be at risk. If you suffer from ill health, your prospects for a speedy recovery could be harmed by added worry about your employment position. So it helps to know where you stand legally.

Check your contract; it may have something to say on the subject of absence. Service agreements sometimes include a provision entitling the company to dismiss in the event of long-term incapacity. Clause 9(d) in the sample agreement in Appendix 1 is a typical example. But even if the contract specifically caters for termination in defined circumstances, you should still be vigilant to ensure that you are given a fair deal. The ACAS handbook *Discipline at Work* again gives helpful guidance.

The terms of any company sick pay scheme also need to be considered. It is not, however, automatically unfair to dismiss an employee while he remains eligible for sick pay under the rules of the scheme. Nor is it inevitably fair to dismiss someone once his rights pursuant to any such scheme are exhausted.

Occasionally, employers argue that a prolonged illness 'frustrates' the contract, so that the job comes to an end through operation of the law as a result of the unforeseen occurrence of the sickness, without there being a dismissal. Guidelines in this area were laid down in the case of *Marshall v Harland & Wolff Ltd* (1972). The following points are likely to be relevant:

1. the terms of your contract;
2. how long the employment was going to last in the absence of

sickness (a short-term contract is more likely to be frustrated than a job expected to last for the foreseeable future);
3. the nature of the job – if it is a key post, frustration is more of a risk;
4. the nature of the illness or injury, how long it has already continued and your prospects for recovery;
5. your length of service.

A court or tribunal will be reluctant to conclude that your contract has been frustrated. This is just as well, since such a decision will deprive you of the legal rights that you would have if you were dismissed.

11.2 Special cases

Disability
If you are registered as a disabled person, you are entitled to special consideration from your employer. It will not be easy for him to justify dismissing you because of any lack of capability on your part where that could have been anticipated when you were originally offered the job.

The Disabled Persons Registration Act 1944 provides that a disabled person cannot be dismissed (unless there is 'reasonable cause' for so doing) if that would reduce the number of disabled workers in the business to below the fixed quota of 3 per cent. The quota is ignored too often in British industry, but this stipulation does at least give you some extra security.

If, nevertheless, your job does come under threat, perhaps because you suffer disablement which makes fulfilling your original job description very difficult, it may be worth urging your employer to consider whether your duties can be revised so that you can cope and continue to make a worthwhile contribution to the success of the business. The local Disablement Resettlement Officer may also be able to help with constructive advice.

Work-related ill health
Some working environments can cause or exacerbate illness or injury. Fortunately, this is rare in the case of employees of executive status. If such a problem does arise there is naturally a heavy onus on the company to rectify the adverse conditions, and dismissal for sickness absence should only be a last resort.

On the other hand, it might occasionally be fair to dismiss even if illness is just a risk. This could happen in a high-stress job where the executive concerned has a history of heart trouble. But in order to justify termination of your services on this basis, the employer would certainly have to go to great lengths to treat you in a caring and reasonable manner.

Pregnancy
It is unfair (and may also be sex discrimination) to dismiss a woman because she is pregnant, or for any other reason connected with her pregnancy, unless:

1. at the dismissal date she is incapable because of her pregnancy of doing the work which she is employed to do; or
2. she cannot after that date, and because of her pregnancy, continue to do that work without contravening a statute.

The law does not provide a definition of the phrase 'any other reason connected with pregnancy'. It is wide enough to be liberally interpreted and would cover pregnancy-related illness, miscarriages and abortions.

Even if one of the two exceptions applies, dismissal will still be unfair if at the time of the dismissal there was a suitable alternative vacancy which was not offered in accordance with the detailed requirements of the employment protection legislation.

11.3 Consultation and investigation

Having your say
Employers should avoid making snap decisions in cases of sickness absence. If you are ultimately dismissed and present a claim to the industrial tribunal, the basic question will be whether, in all the circumstances, the employer could have been expected to wait any longer before taking positive action.

In order to strike a fair balance between protecting the company's commercial interests and behaving responsibly towards an unwell member of staff, management must obtain sufficient information about the medical position.

You should therefore be asked directly about your state of health. Over the years, courts and tribunals have fought shy of laying down detailed procedural guidance. They have pointed out that the correct approach will depend upon the particular facts involved. The general underlying principle was stated by the Employment Appeal Tribunal in *East Lindsay District Council v Daubney* (1977):

Discussion and consultation will often bring to light facts ... of which the employers were unaware, and which will throw new light on the problem. Or the employee may wish to seek medical advice on his own account, which, brought to the notice of the employers' medical advisers, will cause them to change their opinion. There are many possibilities. Only one thing is certain, and that is that if the employee is not consulted, and given an opportunity to state his case, an injustice may be done.

Take advantage of any chance for discussion, especially if you are able to give your employer a date in the not too distant future when you realistically expect to be fit enough to resume work.

Medical opinions
Neither you nor your employer is likely to be a medical expert. Yet while the ultimate decision on your future involves a fair assessment of the industrial realities rather than a precise medical diagnosis, the quotation above shows the importance of seeking a doctor's prognosis.

The answer that a doctor gives may depend upon the way in which the question is framed. He might justifiably refuse to guarantee a full return to health in the near future yet still be prepared, if asked, to express a reasonable degree of confidence about your recovery prospects which should be enough to satisfy many employers.

You may lack confidence in the company doctor and, equally, the management may be sceptical about an encouraging report from your own GP. The solution could be to arrange an independent examination. In some cases, it may be necessary to call in a specialist.

No one can force you to undergo a medical examination (although if the contract provides for one, you will risk serious disciplinary action by refusing to comply with an order to go for a check-up). Your employer should also explain to you your rights under the Access to Medical Reports Act 1988 – which include the right to refuse to allow disclosure of the report to him. But before deciding not to co-operate, you should bear in mind that this could mean the company has to reach a decision on the basis of inadequate information. You may suffer unnecessarily as a result if, for example, you are fairly dismissed on the available data when a thorough examination might have revealed that you would soon be fit again.

Inevitably, there are times when professionals disagree among themselves. Your employer may be faced with conflicting advice if, for instance, the company doctor and your own take different views of your condition. Unfortunately, it may be legitimate for a company to make its decision on the strength of the opinion which is less favourable to you. In such a case, the degree of risk involved in retaining you, both to the business and yourself, will be an important factor.

11.4 The decision

Your employer's reaction to your ill health will be governed by a variety of considerations, such as:

1. the type of illness;
2. how it was caused;
3. its expected duration;
4. the nature of your job;
5. whether replacing you is an urgent commercial necessity;
6. the effect of your absence on other employees;
7. your length of service.

Because there are so many variables in the equation, it is inevitable that management has some discretion as to how much weight it attaches to any point in a particular case.

Even if it is not possible for you to return to your original duties in the near future, there may still be a part that you can usefully play in the organisation. One practical point that might be worth talking over during the consultation process is whether there are any alternative posts for which you are suitable. If retirement is not too far away, you might actually welcome the prospect of an easing of the pressure, while still contributing your experience and business know-how in a modified role. Although companies are not expected to go to unreasonable lengths to accommodate someone who is not able to carry out his job to the full extent, an employer who disregards altogether the possibility of finding you some other position and is unwilling to consider any other form of compromise may be vulnerable to an unfair dismissal claim.

11.5 Persistent intermittent absenteeism

Where there is no chronic medical problem, poor attendance is less of a problem with executives than it is with junior employees. It is worth mentioning, all the same, that a time will come when a frequent absentee can be fairly dismissed and that a failure to consult him at the time of dismissal will not necessarily mean that the company will be powerless to resist an unfair dismissal claim.

A clear statement of the key factors was made by the Employment Appeal Tribunal in *International Sports Co Ltd v Thomson* (1980):

> It would be placing too heavy a burden on an employer to require him to carry out a formal medical investigation and, even if he did, such an investigation would rarely be fruitful because of the transient nature of the employee's symptoms and complaints. What is required . . . is, firstly, that there should be a fair review by the employer of the attendance record and the reasons for it; and, secondly, appropriate warnings, after the employee has been given an opportunity to make representations. If then there is no adequate improvement in the attendance record, it is likely that in most cases the employer will be justified in treating the persistent absences as a sufficient reason for dismissing the employee.

11.6 Maternity leave

A woman who has at least two years' service as at the beginning of the eleventh week prior to the expected week of confinement qualifies for maternity leave. She must, however, comply with a number of detailed (and by no means straightforward) requirements contained within the Consolidation Act, which also stipulates precisely how she must exercise her right to return to work after the baby is born. Suffice it to say here that the law in this area has been roundly condemned by the courts as being of 'inordinate complexity exceeding the worst excesses of a taxing statute'.

An employer must allow a woman who has complied with the statutory procedures to return to her original job on terms and conditions no less favourable than those which would have applied if she had not been absent. It need not be exactly the same work but must be of the same nature and capacity and at the same place. If, as is becoming increasingly common, the contract gives a female executive maternity leave rights which are more generous than the minimum legal requirement, the employer must of course comply with those terms.

Maternity leave does not break one's period of continuous employment and indeed it counts as part of that period. Thus the absence does not reduce accrued rights to redundancy pay or to notice entitlement.

A company which does not allow a woman to return to work after maternity leave is regarded (save in a few exceptional circumstances described in the small print of the legislation) as having dismissed her. Such a dismissal is not automatically unfair, but in practice it will usually be so.

Chapter 12

Disciplinary Complaints

12.1 The problem

Nothing is more likely to damage your career than an accusation of misconduct. The best policy is to try not to be placed in a position where you risk serious criticism on account of your behaviour. Familiarising yourself with your contractual duties and the company's rules and regulations is therefore an essential first step in the survival process.

It would be naive, though, to think that every disciplinary complaint is avoidable. You may find yourself in dispute with management on what seems to you to be a fundamental point of principle. Perhaps even worse, you might be subjected to a disciplinary inquiry when you believe that you have done nothing wrong. If this happens, your job could still be just as much in jeopardy in the long run as that of an employee who has clearly and inexcusably committed an offence.

The law helps - at least up to a point - to make sure you get a fair deal if a disciplinary problem does arise. Courts and tribunals acknowledge that you are entitled to 'natural justice', ie that:

1. you should be told the details of the complaint against you;
2. you should be given a chance to state your case;
3. your employer should act in good faith.

The Employment Appeal Tribunal has said that it is impossible to itemise every circumstance that amounts to a breach of natural justice, while making it clear that, for example, a manager should not normally act both as 'witness and judge' in the procedure leading to a decision to dismiss.

Again, there is likely to be a serious breach of natural justice if a manager, after hearing an employee's case at a disciplinary interview or appeal meeting, has a private discussion with the person who presented the case on behalf of the company, or with a witness, before reaching his decision. To act in such a way is wrong because the employee may be denied a full opportunity to respond to every point being made against him.

Practical guidelines on the way in which an allegation of misconduct ought to be handled are available in the ACAS Code of Practice on disciplinary and other employment procedures, and in the handbook *Discipline at Work*.

The Code says, for instance, that:

> When a disciplinary matter arises, the supervisor or manager should first establish the facts promptly before recollections fade, taking into account the statements of any available witness. In serious cases, consideration should be given to a brief period of suspension while the case is investigated and this suspension should be with pay.

It is equally important that disciplinary proceedings should not become unduly protracted. In extreme cases, unjustified delay can render a dismissal unfair even in a case where a similar penalty would have been legitimate had management not dragged its feet.

While the recommendations of the Code may not have to be followed in every case, tribunals hearing unfair dismissal claims are entitled to take note of any breach of the Code. Certainly, a fair-minded employer should not ignore the ACAS recommendations without good reason.

Disobedience

Suppose you object to carrying out a particular management order. What can you do and will defiance cost you your job?

The law is clear. You are obliged to obey a reasonable instruction given by an authorised superior. This is made explicit in most sets of disciplinary rules, but is in any event a term built in to your contract by the common law. Blatant disobedience is normally classed as gross misconduct justifying summary dismissal, ie without notice.

When a confrontation occurs, the first question is whether the instruction is reasonable. Arguments about what exactly you can be required to do may be resolved by careful study of the small print of your contract. Remember that it is not only a refusal to perform your normal duties which can amount to gross misconduct. If your employer has the right, for example, to insist that you undertake certain other tasks or to move you to another department, your job will be at risk if you dig in your heels and disobey.

Although the terms of your contract are therefore highly relevant, you should be careful about relying too heavily on what has been agreed in the past as grounds for objecting to a new order. Tribunals accept that an employee can sometimes be fairly dismissed for declining to do something which falls outside the scope of his existing contract, for example if, without good cause, he refuses during a business emergency to help out when it was realistic to ask him to do so. The company should not act too hastily, however, and should make clear the consequences of continued intransigence.

Conversely, you may be entitled to disobey an instruction which management ostensibly has the power to give. You cannot be compelled to commit, or be a party to, a criminal offence or to undertake any other unlawful act (such as, in one reported case, procuring prostitutes for the firm's customers), nor can you be forced to put yourself in immediate physical danger. When the Irish troubles peaked in the 1970s, it was suggested that an employee based in England might be able to decline to go to Belfast on company business, even though his contract provided for that.

Equally, you may have a right of redress if you are dismissed for failure to comply with an unjust order. The classic case in this area, *Payne v Spook Erection Ltd* (1984), involved a foreman who was 'fully justified in law' in declining to implement a bizarre and patently unfair scheme for monitoring his subordinates.

Your state of health can be significant if disobedience is alleged. A reasonable employer would not, for example, be entitled to instruct a man who has just resumed work following a major heart attack to undertake immediately a long and arduous period of foreign travel. But illness will not excuse disobedience to a legitimate order if you can indeed comply with what is required.

Breach of discipline

Any written disciplinary rules that affect you deserve careful study. They will probably list examples of gross misconduct, such as:

1. theft, unauthorised possession of or wanton damage to property belonging to the company, its employees or customers;
2. acts of violence during working hours;
3. drunkenness during working hours;
4. unauthorised disclosure of confidential information;
5. working for or assisting a competitor.

The catalogue of offences regarded as serious enough to merit dismissal for a single occurrence is sometimes lengthy. Most employers also take the precaution of stating that the illustrations given are not exhaustive. If you commit an act which is specifically prohibited, you may lose your job even if what you have done is not usually regarded as quite so reprehensible in other organisations. Entering into an adulterous relationship with a colleague is an example. On the other hand, if your employer fails to adopt a particular rule, he might find it difficult to dismiss you summarily for breach of it. An ambiguous rule will carry much less weight than a specific one.

Important as rules are, they do not necessarily bite with the same degree of force in every case. Summary dismissal may not be in breach of contract (ie you will be unlikely to succeed if you sue for pay for your notice period) and yet still unfair if your employer behaves unreasonably by, for example:

(a) applying the rules inconsistently; or
(b) ignoring extenuating factors; or
(c) refusing to allow you to appeal.

Conversely, it is possible for a dismissal which is technically in breach of contract (ie a summary dismissal when notice should have been given) to be fair. In short, everything depends upon the seriousness of the particular incident in question and upon the significance of the surrounding circumstances. What is vital is that no employer should approach disciplinary problems with a closed mind.

Offences away from work

Sometimes it is unclear whether misconduct is sufficiently linked to the job to entitle the employer to take disciplinary action. Mishaps at social functions such as Christmas parties are a typical source of problems. But if an incident has occurred involving violence or which leads to a soured atmosphere at work, management may consider that it has little option but to take action.

ACAS has long recommended that criminal offences outside employment should not be treated as automatic reasons for dismissal. The main consideration ought to be whether the offence is one which makes the employee unsuitable for his or her type of work or unacceptable to colleagues.

While a conviction for dishonesty will not invariably justify dismissal, it is more likely to do so in the case of a senior executive in whom a high level of trust is invested.

If you are banned from driving and using your car is a vital part of your job, your dismissal may be justified. But whether or not the contract has anything to say on this subject, an employer should at least explore the possible alternatives to dismissal, such as allowing you to make other transport arrangements or seeing if you can be fitted in elsewhere within the organisation.

Suspected misconduct
Each year, a number of employees suffer the galling experience of being subjected to disciplinary proceedings for misconduct which they deny having committed.

If you have the misfortune to be wrongly suspected of an offence, the grim reality is that employment law contains fewer safeguards for the incorrectly accused than does criminal law. The familiar principle that the guilt of a person on trial must be proved beyond reasonable doubt does not apply where your job is concerned. If you bring an unfair dismissal claim in the hope of, among other things, 'clearing your name', you may be disappointed. The industrial tribunal, in judging the fairness of your employer's actions, will often ask itself whether he:

1. had a genuine and honest belief that you were guilty;
2. had reasonable grounds for that belief;
3. carried out a reasonable investigation;
4. applied an appropriate penalty.

If the answer to all four questions is 'yes', then your complaint will normally be rejected. There are even rare cases when the employer accepts that you might be innocent and yet is entitled to dismiss you. This will be so where he is reasonably satisfied that one of a group of two or more people, including yourself, must have committed an act of gross misconduct (such as theft of money from a room to which only a very limited number of individuals had access), and yet he cannot pinpoint the actual culprit, despite having examined all the evidence thoroughly.

In other words, the 'unfairness' in an unfair dismissal tends to be of a procedural, rather than a moral, nature.

12.2 Fair procedures

With that in mind, how can you influence your employer's decision on your fate? In the hope of getting a fair deal, you should press him to undertake the most careful inquiry into the facts. Too often, even in serious cases, the investigative process is skimped. Make sure that management is fully aware of your version of events and of any points to which you think it should pay special attention.

If the person handling the matter seems to be relying on information given to him by others, it is worth pressing for full and frank disclosure of what they have said and for sight of any written statements or other relevant documents that may have been prepared. You may even wish the witnesses to be called into the meeting, so that you can question them yourself.

While you should be offered the right to be accompanied at a disciplinary hearing by a fellow employee or (if appropriate) by a trade union representative, you might prefer your solicitor to be present. There is no universal rule that you are always entitled to professional legal representation in the absence of a specific right in the company rules. High-powered support will often be unnecessary. In exceptional cases, though, such as those in which dishonesty is alleged, it may make sense to press the point strongly.

It is often a good idea to write up your own notes of a disciplinary interview immediately afterwards. If you later disagree with the company about what was said at the time, having your own record could prove invaluable.

Warnings

Unless you are guilty of gross misconduct, it will seldom be fair to dismiss you for a first breach of discipline. Proper procedures should indicate that warnings will be given for minor offences.

An initial warning is often verbal, even if logged in writing for record purposes. A further complaint may lead to a written warning, which will sometimes be described as final. If intended as a last step prior to dismissal, such a warning should describe the nature of the offence and make it clear that a repetition will cause you to be dismissed. A final warning ought not to be worded vaguely. You are entitled to know what will happen if you transgress again. If you are not told of the risk that you run, you might be able to complain of an unfair dismissal if you are sacked following a recurrence of the same conduct.

If you are given a written warning, you may be asked to sign a copy to acknowledge receipt. There is little to be gained from refusing to do so, but if you object to the warning for some reason, you should make that clear and pursue your rights under the appeals procedure.

Arguably, there is less of a need for formal warnings where senior employees are concerned. By the nature of your job, you may reasonably be expected to be aware of the standards that are required. Even so, dismissal should never come as a bolt from the blue, however exalted your place in the corporate hierarchy.

You need to know how long any warning will last. If neither the disciplinary rules nor the warning itself provide this information, ask what is intended. It would not be fair for the warning to remain in force for an excessive period. The length of time for which the warning stays on record depends in most cases upon the seriousness of the offence. A procedure which keeps alive a warning (even for a major breach of discipline) for more than two or three years is almost always unjust. Twelve months is usually a more appropriate period.

Alternative sanctions
Warnings or dismissal are not the only possible penalties for misconduct. Your employer may look at a variety of alternative sanctions. If he does not, you may even wish to suggest one of them yourself, in circumstances where it seems a lesser evil than a final warning or dismissal.

The possibilities include:

1. suspension with pay;
2. suspension on reduced pay;
3. unpaid suspension;
4. demotion;
5. transfer;
6. loss of privileges.

Appeals
You may be dissatisfied with a disciplinary decision for any one of a number of reasons. You may deny having done anything wrong at all. Even if you admit to being at fault, you may wish management to take fuller account of mitigating factors or to impose a lesser punishment. It may also be that further relevant information comes to light after the original decision was taken which, in your opinion, means that management should reconsider its attitude.

The company rules should lay down an appeals procedure. If they do so, and you are nevertheless denied the right to appeal, that could render an otherwise justified dismissal unfair. If nothing is specified, it is still important to discover what steps are open to you to challenge your employer's judgment.

The appeal ought to be dealt with by someone who was not

directly involved in taking the original decision. It is usually only fair to deny you a right to appeal if top management has already been closely concerned in the matter because of your senior status or because the business is so small that there is no one left to whom you can bring your complaint.

The principles of fair procedure which govern the conduct of disciplinary hearings also apply, by and large, to appeal hearings. Do not be deterred from exercising your right of appeal by the belief that the outcome will be a foregone conclusion. If (admittedly, in some companies it is a big 'if') your employer is genuinely concerned to make sure you have a fair deal, it is quite possible that the original decision will be reversed, or at least modified, upon appeal.

Chapter 13

Are You Redundant?

13.1 Job insecurity

Redundancy is a word which many executives dread. To be described as surplus to requirements, perhaps after many years of loyal and diligent service, can cripple the self-esteem of even the most resilient person.

The past decade has seen labour-shedding on a massive scale. Manufacturing industry has been especially hard hit, but even sunrise companies specialising in new technology have at times found it necessary to prune their work-force. Redundancies have by no means been restricted to those nearing the end of their careers or whose job performance has been subject to criticism. During the past decade, it has become increasingly clear that few people can count on having a job for life.

Losing your job as a result of a redundancy programme will often be a demoralising blow from which it is difficult to recover. If you are over 50 years of age, if your skills are not in demand or if you live in an economic blackspot, you may find that your chances of finding a suitable job elsewhere are poor.

Fortunately, you are not always powerless when redundancies are threatened. Apart from any safeguards built into your employment contract, you may be eligible for statutory rights not to be unfairly dismissed and to redundancy pay calculated on the basis of a formula reflecting your age, years of service and (up to a point) salary level.

Ironic as it may seem today, modern redundancy law developed from the belief in the 1960s that a state scheme was needed as an incentive to job mobility at a time of chronic labour shortage. Harold Wilson's government introduced the original Redundancy Payments

Act 1965, which gave redundant workers the right for the first time to a statutory severance payment if they satisfied certain qualifying conditions. The scheme was subsidised by the taxpayer in the granting to employers of a sizeable rebate on each statutory redundancy payment made.

Changes in the economy and in the make-up of industry have stood the logic of the original legislation on its head. The rebate has now been scrapped. Even so, businesses large and small continue to find it necessary to cut jobs. The commercial difficulties which necessitate those cuts may cause management to underestimate the need to keep their employees' interests at heart. To get a fair deal you need to be fully aware of your legal entitlements and the extent to which you can influence your own destiny.

13.2 What is redundancy?

The legal background

The phrase 'redundancy situation' is commonly used, both in industry and in the courtroom, but it appears nowhere in the relevant legislation. When job losses are in prospect, it is easy to lose sight of the precise legal position, but for you to be genuinely redundant, your case must fall within the definition of redundancy contained in the Consolidation Act.

While redundancy rights can sometimes arise in the context of men being laid off from work or put on short time, in the case of a business executive, redundancy almost always involves a dismissal. Briefly, you may be dismissed for redundancy when one of the following events occurs or is expected to occur:

1. the business closes;
2. the business moves;
3. the job disappears.

When the business closes or moves

If the firm that you work for closes down, it will usually be beyond dispute that you are redundant. However, if the reason for the closure is that your employer has transferred his business to someone else, there may be no dismissal because you have been automatically transferred to work for the new owner (see below).

Where the location of the business changes, the terms of your contract will be important. If you are subject to an express or implied mobility clause, which covers the move to a new base, the mere closure of the office or factory where you work at present will not in itself give rise to redundancy.

Where there is no mobility clause, the position is different. If your employer ceases business at every place where you can be required to work under your contract, you will be redundant.

Has your job really disappeared?
Redundancies arising from a reduction in work present more difficult questions. Until a few years ago, it seemed clear that there was redundancy where an employer no longer required the same number of employees. However, as a result of a case in which a determined executive fought a long battle through the courts, the position now appears to be more complicated than was once thought.

The facts of *Cowen v Haden Carrier Ltd* (1982) were quite simple. Mr Cowen was promoted from the position of regional surveyor to that of divisional contracts surveyor. Later, his employers decided to reduce the number of staff employed. Mr Cowen was not willing to accept demotion and was dismissed. He argued that he was not redundant because there was other work available within the terms of his contract of employment. The Employment Appeal Tribunal accepted his argument, albeit reluctantly, saying that, in the experience of the members deciding the case, in practice a redundancy 'is accepted as having been shown where it is demonstrated that the actual job which the claimant was carrying out had ceased to exist'.

The Court of Appeal overruled the decision on the facts, but not this interpretation of the general law. It therefore seems to be necessary to look carefully at the contract terms before deciding whether or not there is redundancy. Possibly it is not too much of an exaggeration to say that the more flexibility your employer retains in framing your job duties, the harder he may find it to argue that you are redundant.

Bumping
'Bumping', which is sometimes referred to as 'transferred' or 'translated' redundancy, is a well-recognised industrial practice. It takes place where an employee's work disappears, but he is retained and another employee is dismissed instead.

The law provides that the business of your employer and that of any associated employer are to be treated as one for redundancy law purposes, if appropriate. So, if the business in which you work is expanding, but an associated employer's business slims down and a long-serving employee of that other business is transferred to work for your company, resulting in your dismissal, you may be redundant. This is so despite the fact that your own company is not suffering from a reduction in work.

Reorganisational redundancy
It was long thought that a mere redistribution of duties without any reduction in the total number of employees required or the total amount of work to be done did not amount to redundancy.

It is now clear that this was too simplistic a view. Take the example of a company implementing new technology which requires the recruitment of an employee with a new skill. His job might necessarily include some or all of the functions formerly performed by existing employees, such as yourself. If, as a result, your company no longer requires your services, your dismissal might be due to redundancy.

Spreading or subcontracting the work
There may be a redundancy even when your company's requirements for work of a particular kind to be done remain the same. This will be so if the same work is done by fewer employees or by no employees at all.

Thus, as part of a cost-cutting exercise, an employer may simply ask some of the existing employees doing a job to absorb the work of colleagues who are then no longer required and are consequently made redundant.

A popular means of saving costs is to reduce the work-force and hire outside contractors to perform the same duties. Employees dismissed in the wake of such an exercise will usually be redundant.

Non-redundancy dismissals
By no means every dismisal occasioned by the need to restructure the business or to make economies is due to redundancy. If the reason for dismissal is your employer's desire to run the business cost-effectively and not because of any reduction in the number of employees needed to carry out your particular functions, you will not be redundant.

If you are employed under a fixed-term contract which comes to an end and is not renewed, you may be redundant. Occasionally, this may be foreseen even at the start of your employment: for example, if your position is subject to funding from an outside source or if you are taken on to supervise a particular contract, as may happen in the engineering and construction fields amongst others. However, if you are replaced by another employee, say of a lower grade and commanding less pay, there is unlikely to be a redundancy.

Business transfers
If your employer's trade or business is sold, your job rights will depend upon whether or not the Transfer of Undertakings (Protection of Employment) Regulatons of 1981 are applicable. Unfortunately the Regulations, which do not apply where all that happens is a sale of shares in a limited company, are extremely complex.

To summarise, the Regulations come into play when there is a relevant transfer, ie:

1. a transfer of a business or part of a business (usually including a transfer of its goodwill) from one employer to another; where
2. the business is located in the UK and is run as a commercial venture.

If you are employed in the business at the time of the transfer, you will become employed by the purchaser and you should not be redundant. In the important case of *Litster v Forth Dry Dock & Engineering Co Ltd* (1989), the House of Lords rejected an argument which would have reduced the value of the Regulations as a means of preserving jobs. It had been suggested that the Regulations did not apply if a business purchaser arranged with the buyer to sack employees in the business a short time before it was sold. This would have left many people with worthless claims against insolvent companies. But the Law Lords, applying European law, ruled that liability for a dismissal by a seller before a business transfer passes to the purchaser if the employee has been unfairly dismissed for a reason connected with the transfer.

13.3 When redundancy is in the air

Responding to a warning
A fair-minded employer will, unless circumstances are exceptional, give affected employees plenty of advance warning about possible redundancies. He will consult with the candidates for redundancy and their trade union representatives, if any, about his proposals and will explore possible alternatives to job cuts. Failure to give you a fair deal in this respect is likely to expose a company to legal attack.

When planned job reductions are announced, it is easy to panic, even if words of reassurance are added. When redundancies are in the air, though, you need to keep your head. Although there may be a great temptation to seek alternative employment at the earliest opportunity, you should weigh up considerations such as:

1. how likely it is that you personally will be affected by the cutbacks;
2. whether this is only a temporary down-turn which may in the end not necessitate redundancies on the scale now envisaged;
3. whether you may forfeit valuable legal rights if you leave too soon.

The danger that, by trying to protect your future career prospects, you may throw away substantial cash sums in terms of severance payments is a real one, as the case of *International Computers Ltd v Kennedy* (1981) illustrates. In October 1979, the company announced that a factory was to close by the end of September 1980. Employees were advised to make every effort to find other jobs as quickly as possible. Negotiations had yet to be concluded with the trade unions as to the timing of the redundancies, but Ms Kennedy quickly found another job. She left and sought a redundancy payment. Her claim failed because no date had been fixed for the ending of her employment. As was said in an earlier case, an employee in this position:

> ... has a perfectly secure right if he thinks fit to wait until his contract is determined, to take his redundancy payment, and then see what he can do in regard to finding other employment. If he does ... choose to leave his existing employment before the last minute in order to look for a new job before the rush of others competing with him comes, then that is up to him.

This quotation shows the gulf between strict legal principles and industrial reality. But the lesson of the Kennedy case is that if you have the chance to take another job before your redundancy has been confirmed, you may have to choose between safeguarding your future and cashing in on the job rights built up over the years in your present employment.

Volunteering for redundancy

The hard choice between premature resignation and awaiting redundancy does not apply if you are offered the right to volunteer for redundancy. The courts have made it clear that an employee who responds to an employer's initiative by volunteering to go is not resigning, but making himself available to be dismissed. As a result, a volunteer remains entitled to his statutory right to redundancy pay.

Early retirement

Contrastingly, if you take the initiative by seeking early retirement, perhaps because you are in poor health, you may not have redundancy rights. For example, an employer who envisages having to slim down his work-force in the future, perhaps after introducing new technology, may offer those who are prepared to resign rather than to wait to volunteer for redundancy a financial inducement, perhaps exceeding state redundancy pay. If there is no element whatsoever of coercion in the deal, there will be no dismissal if you accept such an offer.

13.4 Offers of alternative employment

If your employer tells you that you can be relocated elsewhere within the business, there should be no question of dismissal if the change falls within the existing terms of your employment. This will be the case if, for example, you are asked to perform the same job at the same rate of pay but at a different office or factory and the move is catered for by a mobility clause in your contract.

You may lose your redundancy payment rights if, among other matters, you unreasonably refuse an offer of suitable alternative employment. This is so even if the alternative job offered involves a change in your terms of contract or is with an associated employer, such as another company which is controlled, in terms of shareholders' voting power, by the same person or people who control the company that you work for. The details of the offer must be made clear; the mere expression of optimism that a job can be found is not enough.

There is a close link between the vexed questions of whether an offer of employment is 'suitable' and whether a refusal is 'unreasonable'.

As a broad rule of thumb, the more similar the new job is to the old, the more likely the new job is to be suitable. Specific relevant factors concerning the new job may include:

1. whether it involves a loss of status, like reduction in authority or superiority or loss of promotion prospects;
2. pay and benefits;
3. the nature of the new working environment;
4. the new location;
5. the new hours of work.

Whether or not a refusal is unreasonable is more likely to depend upon subjective factors concerning you personally, such as your age, health and domestic circumstances, particularly if the latter mean that changes in your hours or place of work are unacceptable. So it might be possible for a 50-year-old with a heart condition to be acting reasonably if he turned down a job involving more stress and daily travel, whereas a 30-year-old executive with no personal problems who rejected the same offer might forfeit his claim to statutory redundancy pay.

If you accept the offer of a new job on the same terms as your original job then:

(a) you are regarded as not having been made redundant at all;
(b) there is no trial period (see below);
(c) you are not entitled to a redundancy payment; and
(d) you have continuity of employment throughout the period of your original job and the new job.

If you accept the offer of a new job on changed terms, a trial period comes into effect automatically. It will normally be for four weeks from the time when you start to work under the new contract. It can be extended for the specific purpose of retraining you for new work provided that any agreement to do so:

- is made before you start work under the new contract;
- is in writing;
- specifies the date at the end of the trial period; and
- specifies the terms of employment which will apply as at the end of that period.

If you end the contract for any reason during the trial period, you will be treated as having been dismissed on the date when your original job ended. Your entitlement to redundancy pay will depend on the factors referred to above, just as it will if you are dismissed during the trial period for a reason connected with the changed terms of employment. If you are dismissed for some other reason unconnected with redundancy, you will have to consider whether the circumstances justify an unfair dismissal claim. This question is explored further in the next chapter.

Chapter 14

Redundancy Selection and Consultation

14.1 Why have you been selected?

Any employee who is told that he must lose his job through no fault of his own is likely to ask, 'Why me?' You are entitled to a clear, logical and convincing answer to that question. Above all, you need to satisfy yourself that the decision, however hard, was not taken arbitrarily.

Sometimes redundancy selection is automatically unfair. This will be so where selection is for a 'trade union reason', such as refusing to become or remain a member of a particular trade union; or if you have been unjustifiably selected in contravention of a customary agreement or agreed procedure in respect of redundancies.

Where business executives are concerned, though, management has in most cases considerable discretion in deciding whom to retain and whom to release in a redundancy exercise. Provided your employer acts reasonably, you will find it difficult to launch an effective legal challenge of his decision. Even so, it is worth investigating his approach in detail, since employers do sometimes make erroneous assumptions during the redundancy process which amount to acting unreasonably.

14.2 The selection group

The first question is whether your employer has adopted an appropriate unit of selection for redundancy purposes. Here again, the terms of your contract will be important. Management ought to look at the work that you do and that you could be asked to do under any contractual 'flexibility' provisions before finally deciding upon the groups of people from which redundancy candidates will be sought.

If the business has different sections or different sites, you should enquire whether all its employees have been considered for redundancy or whether your particular part of the operation is the only one which has come under scrutiny for cut-backs. There are no firm legal rules about the proper approach that a company should adopt, but often it will be reasonable to look at the organisation as a whole, without dividing it into separate compartments. Nonetheless, many employers wish to concentrate for redundancy purposes upon only a particular segment of the work-force. If so, ask them how they can justify such action.

14.3 Selection factors

You may be one of a number of employees with a roughly comparable job. If you are being selected for redundancy in preference to one or more of your colleagues, it is worth trying to find out why.

If an employer is committed to an agreed procedure or customary arrangement regarding redundancies, he should adhere to it. If he departs from it when imposing redundancies, he will usually be acting unfairly.

Where business executives are concerned, employers tend to have considerable discretion in the way that they implement redundancies. They are entitled to take into account a variety of selection factors. But any criteria used must be objective, not subjective, so as, according to the Employment Appeal Tribunal:

> ... to ensure that redundancy is not used as a pretext for getting rid of employees which some manager wishes to get rid of for some quite other reasons, eg ... by reason of personal dislike.

It is not possible to draw up an exhaustive list of matters that may legitimately be taken into account. Those referred to below are often considered.

Length of service
'Last in, first out' is a selection procedure frequently agreed with trade unions. In any event, an employer's obligations to act fairly towards his longer-serving employees will mean that length of service is always an important factor in the selection process and will frequently be decisive.

Redundancy, however, will often imply a major organisational change in the business, in which case other factors may have to be considered which may cumulatively outweigh length of service in a particular case. Rarely, it may even be unreasonable to select you for redundancy on the basis of length of service, for instance if doing so entails retaining another employee past retiring age when you are much younger and still have plenty to offer.

Job performance etc
In a slimming-down operation, the job performance and skills of the members of the selection group are likely to be relevant in the redundancy selection process. If it is suggested that you are not sufficiently flexible to adapt to the reshaped structure that is envisaged, you may be able to challenge that view if your past record shows a steady upward progression and if you have carried out a wide range of tasks without serious mishaps. Here again, your job file may prove helpful.

Attendance and disciplinary record
If a person retained at your expense has a significantly worse record in terms of attendance or misconduct, it will be worth drawing the matter to your employer's attention to see whether his view changes upon mature reflection.

Personal circumstances
Most employers are reluctant to pay too much attention to personal circumstances, such as marital status or domestic problems when arriving at redundancy decisions. Yet such matters may be relevant in some cases; one particular example is that if you are registered as disabled, you are entitled to special consideration.

Pay levels
Financial considerations are likely to have played an important part in the decision that redundancies are necessary. Your employer may consider it more cost-effective to retain junior employees who are paid less than you. If this is a relevant factor, one point that you may be prepared to discuss during the consultation process is the possibility of taking a pay cut, either on a temporary or permanent basis.

Just as selection criteria must be reasonable, so must they be rationally applied. In particular, you will probably have good reason to complain if your employer departs at the last minute from an approach to the selection process that has previously been announced.

It is quite possible that some selection factors may point towards your retention while others will, in comparison, favour colleagues. In checking to ensure that your employers have striven to strike a fair balance, it could be worth asking whether they have considered drawing up some form of 'points table' or other grading system, by which the relevant matters can be assessed.

14.4 The consultation process

Consultation is, or should be, a key element in a redundancy exercise. Without it, your employer risks making decisions on the basis of inadequate information and you risk losing your job without having been given sufficient opportunity to convince management that you still have something to contribute.

The statutory duty to consult a trade union about redundancies is well known, but both employers and those directly affected tend to be less familiar with what the law has to say about the need for consultation with affected individuals.

14.5 Trade union consultation

Employers are legally obliged to consult representatives of recognised trade unions about their redundancy proposals. Information on a variety of matters, such as the reasons for the proposed job losses and the way in which they are intended to occur, must be disclosed in writing.

The legislation specifies various time limits. For example, if 100 or more jobs are to go, consultation must begin at least 90 days before the first dismissal takes effect. The overriding principle, though, is that consultation must commence at the earliest opportunity.

This is an obligation to consult, not a duty to reach agreement. The legal requirements are not normally too onerous, but an employer who fails to comply with them will be exposed to a claim for a 'protective award'. Such a claim can only be instituted by the union itself and not by the affected employees.

Inadequate communications bedevil many redundancy programmes. Even employers who are punctilious in consulting staff representatives sometimes fail to talk directly to the people whose jobs are at stake. The law reports contain a number of examples where this kind of neglect has led to a successful unfair dismissal claim. Similarly, not every trade union liaises efficiently with its members, even if its officials are trying hard to defend jobs in their negotiations with the company.

You therefore need to press both management and your own representatives (whether a trade union, staff committee or works council) to make sure that they promptly give you adequate information about the progress of discussion. Only in this way can you be confident of a fair deal.

14.6 Individual consultation

If, like many executives, you have no representative to act on your behalf in redundancy negotiations, it is all the more important for there to be detailed discussions between you and your employer about any plans to make you redundant.

The Employment Appeal Tribunal has emphasised that consultation:

> . . . is one of the foundation stones of modern industrial relations practice . . . in the particular sphere of redundancy, good industrial relations practice . . . requires consultation with the redundant employee so that the employer may find out whether the needs of the business can be met in some other way than by dismissal and, if not, what other steps the employer can take to ameliorate the blow to the employee.

A general policy not to consult with employees of, say, a particular grade, runs contrary to good industrial relations. Although the nature of consultation may differ according to whether one is a shop-floor worker or a member of management, the desirability of consultation applies to employees at all levels in the hierarchy.

If you have not been adequately consulted, and a tribunal is satisfied that consultation could have made a difference to the redundancy decision, there is a good chance that you will succeed in an unfair dismissal claim and be entitled to compensation.

Far better, of course, for it not to come to that. The problem is that employers are apt to underestimate the value of direct discussion with executives who figure in their job-cutting plans.

There seem to be three main reasons why employers take a deliberate decision not to consult. First, there may be a view that consultation may do little but depress and demoralise the work-force which is bound to see the implementation of redundancies as a *fait accompli*. Second, in some industries the employer may fear sabotage from disgruntled redundancy candidates. For example, it may be thought that a computer programmer will extract some kind of revenge by introducing a logic bomb into the computer system. Third, the plight of the business may be so grave, and the selection of the individuals concerned so inevitable and so urgently required, that consultation would make absolutely no difference to the outcome.

Non-consultation may be justified on one or more of these grounds, but only in unusual circumstances. An employer who breaks the news of redundancy to you at 4.30 pm on a Friday afternoon, adding that you need not bother to work out your notice, is likely to incur the wrath of most industrial tribunals. Even if he acts in such a way from what he misguidedly thinks are 'humanitarian' reasons, the tribunal will be unlikely to be impressed, as the manner of dismissal would eliminate the possibility, however remote, that following consultation, your job might be saved. Similarly, unless there is evidence that sabotage was a genuine risk, for instance in the light of past experiences with other redundant employees, an argument based on that fear will generally receive short shrift.

Even where vital commercial considerations explain a failure to consult, an employer may be held to have acted unfairly. A typical example occurred in a case when the Employment Appeal Tribunal overturned an industrial tribunal's decision that it was not practicable to consult where 33 redundancies were required urgently, at a time when take-over negotiations were being conducted in secret. The Employment Appeal Tribunal considered that multiple interviews 'could readily have been arranged without inconvenience or dislocation to the company' and that there was insufficient evidence that the need for secrecy precluded consultation.

No firm rules can be laid down as to the form that consultation should take and how long it should last. What matters above all is for the consultation to be a genuine exercise in communciation and not an ill-conceived charade.

As well as asking why you have been selected as a redundancy candidate and, if appropriate, arguing that a fair procedure would result in the selection of one of your colleagues instead, you may find it fruitful to explore the other ways in which the company can achieve the desired savings without putting your job at risk.

The possibilities include:

1. changes in pay structure;
2. relocating you elsewhere within the organisation;
3. a general redistribution of job functions;
4. changes in working patterns.

Above all, you need to take advantage of being given the chance to put your own point of view. A fair employer will already have given thought to the alternatives to redundancy, perhaps even contacting other companies within the same group to see whether vacancies exist elsewhere. If, rather than face unemployment, you would at least be prepared to consider staying on with a reduced salary or a lower level of seniority, you should make that clear. Clearly, if you fail to respond positively to it, the consultation process will achieve little or nothing.

If it seems inevitable that you will have to leave, consultation may still achieve a useful improvement in your severance terms. You might be able, for example, to persuade your employer to give you constructive help by engaging an out-placement counsellor to assist you in finding a new job. Finally, you ought to keep in mind the possibility that circumstances may change between the time when you are first told that you are a redundancy candidate and the date when your employment ends. If the company fails to treat consultation as an ongoing process, it may be treating you unfairly.

An example of this is provided by the case of *Stacey v Babcock Power Ltd* (1986). Mr Stacey was notified in February 1984 that he would be made redundant the following May. In April, the company unexpectedly obtained new contracts which might have made it possible for it to keep him in work. Unfortunately, they allowed his notice to expire without further action and proceeded to recruit new employees. The Employment Appeal Tribunal decided that the failure to offer a long-serving worker the chance to stay on rendered unfair a redundancy which had originally been justified.

Demoralising as the threat of redundancy may be, therefore, all is not necessarily lost even when you are told that you are among those who will have to leave. Although the outlook may seem bleak, a constructive approach towards consultation might result in hitherto unconsidered options coming to light which could enable your job to be saved at the eleventh hour.

Chapter 15

Constructive Dismissal

15.1 What does it mean?

The possibility of claiming that you have been constructively dismissed has already been mentioned several times. But what exactly is constructive dismissal?

Put simply, you are constructively dismissed if your employer breaks an important term of your employment contract. If he does, you will be entitled to walk out of your job and, even though you have not been 'fired', take advantage of the various rights available to a dismissed employee, such as the right to claim that your dismissal was unfair.

Remember that unreasonable behaviour on your employer's part will not amount to constructive dismissal if the contract is not broken. Here is yet another reason why you should clarify as many of your contract terms as possible. If you do not do so, you may be left in some doubt as to when a constructive dismissal occurs.

Naturally, some cases of constructive dismissal are clear-cut. Classic examples are reductions in pay and demotion. But if your company has retained a good deal of discretion on key matters, it may be able to impose major changes on your working life without giving rise to a constructive dismissal claim. For instance, you may be asked to go to a new and different place of work under the provisions of a mobility clause, or have the emphasis of your duties changed significantly, pursuant to a clause in the contract providing for flexible working.

Nor is that all. In order to claim that you have been constructively dismissed, you must show that:

1. your employer has broken your contract; and

2. that action was so fundamental as to justify your ending the contract (or that it was 'the last straw'); and that
3. you left the job as a result of your contract being broken; and that
4. you did not delay too long in leaving.

In practice, you will find that courts and tribunals called upon to decide whether these conditions have been satisfied are themselves able to exercise a considerable degree of discretion.

15.2 Has the contract been broken?

The main area for uncertainty in constructive dismissal cases concerns an apparent breach of an implied term of your contract. Implied terms were discussed in Chapter 2.

You will sometimes find that if your employer acts towards you in an unsatisfactory way, he is in breach of his implied duty of mutual trust and confidence. Employers should not, without good cause, behave in a manner that is likely to destroy or seriously damage the employment relationship.

The law reports provide many illustrations of this kind of conduct. They include:

1. sexual harassment;
2. humiliating you in the presence of your colleagues;
3. turning a blind eye to harassment of you by your colleagues;
4. overworking you and failing to provide you with reasonable support;
5. penalising minor breaches of discipline with disproportionate severity.

The Employment Appeal Tribunal has also made it clear that conduct 'which a literal interpretation of the written words of the contract might appear to justify' may in practice amount to a destruction of the relationship of trust and confidence. This is worth remembering if your employer tries to justify giving you a raw deal by interpreting a stringent contract of employment harshly, eg by insisting you move your place of work at short notice and without financial help – from Leeds to Birmingham, as in one case – even where this is within the terms of an express contractual mobility clause.

Does a failure to give you a pay rise, say on an annual basis, amount to constructive dismissal? You might think the answer would be 'no', but the position is not quite that simple. In *F C*

Gardner Ltd v Beresford (1978), the employee was given no pay increase for two years. Others did receive rises during that time. The Employment Appeal Tribunal thought that in most circumstances it would be reasonable to imply a term along the lines that an employer will not treat his employees 'arbitrarily, capriciously or inequitably' in matters of remuneration. Failure to give you a fair deal in terms of a pay rise can, therefore, amount to constructive dismissal if it reflects victimisation.

Another interesting question is whether you have any right of redress if, while continuing to pay your salary, your employer does not give you any work to do, perhaps sending you home and saying for some reason, 'Don't call us, we'll call you'. If this is not permitted by an express 'garden leave' clause – see Chapter 5 – can you argue that you have been denied 'the right to work'?

There is no general right to work. In a much-quoted phrase, one judge put the position bluntly:

> Provided I pay my cook her wages regularly, she cannot complain if I choose to take any or all of my meals out.

Nevertheless, there are circumstances in which an employer may be under a contractual duty to provide work. Many salesmen, for instance, are in practice entitled to be allowed to work in order to earn their commission.

In other jobs, there may be good reasons why employees have a right, under the contract, to be given work to do. This is true of people working in the entertainment industry, who need to practise their skills regularly. In the industrial context, too, it might be relevant to consider whether your reputation will be damaged if it becomes widely known that you have had your work taken away from you. Broadly speaking, the higher a person is in the management structure, the more essential it is for him or her to be given work when it is available.

There are even one or two hints in the case law that some employees can claim that they have been constructively dismissed if they are denied job satisfaction. Realistically, though, you would need to have strong evidence that the existence of such a right is part of your particular deal with your employer, and that you have been denied satisfaction from your work in a clear and unjustifiable fashion, before you could pursue litigation with confidence.

15.3 How badly has your employer behaved?

You may be able to claim constructive dismissal even if the incident which directly leads to your departure is minor, if it can be regarded as the last straw. If there has been a history of such problems, an industrial tribunal may accept that eventually you became entitled to say 'enough is enough' and leave. Unscrupulous employers are not allowed to squeeze out unwanted executives by indulging in a sustained course of conduct which nevertheless falls short at any particular time of a clear breach of contract.

The general rule, however, is that for you to be justified in ending the relationship, the breach of contract must in itself be serious. A single trivial occurrence does not entitle you to claim that you had been constructively dismissed. A failure to pay your salary at the agreed time, for example, might not in itself amount to constructive dismissal, although if the delay were prolonged or repeated subsequently, the position could be different.

15.4 How to respond

A serious breach of contract by your employer does not itself end your employment. It only gives you the right to choose to do so, should you wish. In order to claim that you have been constructively dismissed, you must give up your job in response to the breaking of your contract.

Simply presenting an unfair dismissal application to an industrial tribunal is not, for instance, sufficient if you continue to report for work. You do not have to give formal written notice that you are leaving, but it is important not to say or do anything which is inconsistent with pursuing a constructive dismissal claim. Certainly, you should make it clear by words or conduct that you are exercising your right to treat yourself as having been dismissed. The best course will often be to confirm the position unambiguously in writing. It may make sense to take professional advice on the wording of an appropriate letter.

While pursuing a complaint through the grievance procedure is sometimes worthwhile, you do not forfeit your right to claim constructive dismissal if you have been treated so badly that you decide that raising the matter through the company's internal procedures will not help you to achieve a fair deal. Nor is it necessarily fatal if you give notice to terminate your contract and work that notice out, rather than walking out on the spot.

Jumping the gun

Do not make the mistake of reacting prematurely when a problem occurs. Unless a serious breach of your contract has taken place, or your employer has made it clear that it will take place, you should not leave in a huff. If you do, your employer will be able to argue that you have simply resigned and not been dismissed.

If you are told, for example, that the company is thinking of implementing a pay cut, but that the decision is not yet definite, that will not in itself be likely to amount to constructive dismissal.

Delaying too long

The other side of the coin is that, when your employer is guilty of a serious breach of your contract, you must not delay your response too long. If you continue to work without leaving, you will eventually lose your right to claim constructive dismissal.

A good example of how this principle operates is provided by the case of *W E Cox Toner (International) Ltd v Crook* (1981). An employee who was reprimanded at the end of July 1980 subsequently demanded, through his solicitors, that the letter of reprimand be withdrawn. On 6 February 1981 he was told that the letter would not be withdrawn. On 3 March 1981 he left. His claim that he had been constructively dismissed failed because of the lapse of time after 6 February 1981 before he took action. However, his failure to leave before 6 February 1981 did not necessarily mean that he had 'waived' the breaking of his contract.

You have a reasonable period of time to decide whether or not to give up your job, but it is not easy to forecast what will be regarded as 'reasonable'. Much will probably depend upon whether you are complaining about a single, unequivocal act, such as suspension in breach of your contract, in which event you ought to respond rapidly, or something such as a gradual change in your status, which may require prolonged consideration. If you work under protest for a limited period of time, your attempts to resolve the dispute through negotiation prior to leaving should not jeopardise your right to claim that you have been constructively dismissed. You should, though, make it clear at all times that you object to the way that you have been treated.

Similarly, if a threat that your contract will be broken is withdrawn, you are not entitled to leave subsequently and claim that you have been constructively dismissed. So, if your company changes its mind about a plan to demote you, but, feeling disgruntled, you still decide to leave, it is likely that you will be regarded as having voluntarily resigned.

15.5 Practical implications

Almost all constructive dismissal cases involve an unfair dismissal claim. You ought to keep in mind, though, that even if you have been constructively dismissed, an industrial tribunal might still regard your employer's actions as fair. Typically, this could occur in the context of a *bona fide* business reorganisation, which involves a change in your terms of employment. If there is a sound business reason for the change and your employer has observed the principles of good industrial relations practice, including full consultation with you and consideration of possible alternative courses, prior to taking action, he will probably have a good defence.

This underlines the importance – before you decide to treat yourself as constructively dismissed and leave your job – of weighing up the pros and cons of so doing.

The first worry is that proving that your contract has been broken may not be easy, particularly if you are complaining about the breach of an unwritten and rather vague term. If you are confident that you can show that your contract has been broken, you might wish to pursue not only an unfair dismissal complaint, but also a claim in respect of breach of your contract. These are potentially valuable rights for many senior executives, but you will do well to remember that litigation is apt to be an uncertain, protracted and depressing business.

Depending upon the kind of problem that has arisen, it may be easier and safer for you to sue for damages for breach of your contract while remaining in your job. You might be able to do this, for example, if you have clearly suffered a direct financial loss. Typically, this will be a realistic option if your pay has been cut for some reason. But if your complaint is that a less tangible term of your employment has been broken, as when you have suffered harassment from your superiors or your status has been eroded, it may be difficult to establish a viable claim for compensation if you do not quit.

Leaving work and consigning yourself to the dole queue is obviously risky. It is easier to find a job when you are in work than out of it. Your age, health and qualifications might be against you. But even if you have another job lined up, a constructive dismissal claim will not always be lucrative. You are obliged to mitigate your losses; this duty is explained in Chapter 18. If you succeed in finding another job, or already have one lined up at the time that you go, it may not be worth suing your employer because the losses for which you could claim reimbursement may be minimal.

In short, for many employees constructive dismissal claims give rise to a Catch 22. If you can afford to leave your job, the claim may not be worth pursuing financially. But if you cannot afford to leave, might it not be better to put up with the treatment that you have received rather than becoming unemployed?

Sometimes, sadly, even a bad deal is better than no deal at all.

Chapter 16

The Threat of Dismissal

16.1 The need for awareness

If your job is threatened, you may be tempted to jump before you are pushed. As an executive with a long-term career plan to protect, you may have sound reasons for leaving before a dismissal occurs or for departing on mutually agreed terms. Rightly or wrongly, mention of a dismissal on your CV will worry many prospective employers.

Sometimes executives have, in effect, a choice as to whether or not to be dismissed. This can happen at a time when you are under pressure and need to make a rapid decision. Even so, you ought to balance the relative advantages and disadvantages of giving up your employment on the one hand, and staying on, with dismissal likely, on the other. Bear in mind that a number of legal avenues may be open to you if you are dismissed and wrongly treated. Those avenues are likely to be closed if, in law, there has been no express or constructive dismissal.

It is also important to avoid drifting, or moving accidentally, into a position in which you are unable to take advantage of dismissal law rights. We have already seen examples of how you may, if you are not careful, forfeit your redundancy rights, the chance to claim constructive dismissal or indeed all your statutory employment rights in the event that your contract is frustrated.

There are a number of other circumstances in which your employer may argue, if it suits him, that you have not been dismissed. You need to be aware of all the possibilities in order to make a realistic decision about the best way of securing your long-term employment and financial position.

16.2 Have you been dismissed?

It is by no means rare for there to be confusion about whether or not a dismissal has actually taken place. Jobs can come to an end in an unorthodox and unplanned way.

This is usually unsatisfactory for all concerned. In the simplest case, you may not be sure whether you should continue to turn up for work or not. Moreover, you need to know if you are eligible for the rights available to a dismissed employee, such as the right to complain of unfair dismissal or to seek a redundancy payment. In theory, it should be easy to tell whether you have left voluntarily or have been dismissed. In reality, the position may be much more complex.

Words of dismissal
Sometimes it is open to doubt whether the language used by your employer, taken in context, amounts to a dismissal. Ambiguous words spoken in anger, or intended merely as a reprimand, may in your eyes amount to words of dismissal, even if there is no constructive dismissal.

Equally, you might use ambiguous words which your superiors treat as a resignation which they will not allow you to retract.

The case law is not wholly consistent, but three basic propositions concerning ambiguous 'resignations' and 'dismissals' are widely accepted, ie:

1. certain words or acts can, as a matter of law, be interpreted only as amounting to a dismissal or resignation;
2. some words or acts are ambiguous and may or may not constitute a dismissal or resignation. Here the question is subjective: did the person hearing the words in fact interpret them as a dismissal or a resignation? If so, there is a dismissal or resignation;
3. if it is not clear how the words were in fact understood, the question is how a reasonable listener would have interpreted them in the particular context. Thus in one case, during an argument, an employee said to his manager, 'I'm leaving, I want my cards'. Those words were capable of constituting a resignation and the manager interpreted them as such. This was therefore a case of resignation.

Nevertheless, all the facts of each case must be considered. For example, if you use the words, 'I am resigning', that unambiguous statement is likely to be taken at face value unless perhaps you are speaking in the heat of the moment or under duress.

In short, you need to watch your words if you do not want to risk jeopardising your job. Equally, if you are not clear about the exact implication of what your employer has told you, it is best to ask him to clarify his meaning.

Ultimatums and warnings
If you leave under duress, you are not resigning. This means that if your employer says, 'Resign or be sacked', that amounts to a dismissal.

The precise interpretation of an ultimatum depends upon the circumstances prevailing at the time. The question for a court or tribunal would be whether your employer's conduct forced you to resign.

As a practical measure, if you regard yourself as having been forced to quit, it is prudent to confirm the position to your employer in writing.

Mutual consent
An employment contract may be brought to an end by the mutual consent of the parties. If so, there will be no dismissal. There is no genuine mutual consent, however, if the deal has in reality been initiated by duress or the threat of dismissal.

Nevertheless, you should once again proceed with caution if you wish to make any claims on the basis that you have been dismissed. An employee discovered this to her cost in the case of *Staffordshire County Council v Donovan* (1981). Ms Donovan worked for a local authority and, during the course of disciplinary proceedings, was told that she would be permitted to terminate her employment on the last day of the year if she so wished. Terms were offered as to suspension on pay and the provision of a reference. Ms Donovan eventually gave notice on this basis, but she later submitted an unfair dismissal application.

The Employment Appeal Tribunal held that this was a case of mutual consent. It pointed out that, where parties seek to negotiate during the course of disciplinary proceedings and an agreed formula is worked out, it would be 'most unfortunate' if the mere fact that agreement was reached while the proceedings continued enabled the employee to say later that there was a dismissal.

Having said that, courts and tribunals are generally vigilant to ensure that an alleged deal bringing a job to a conclusion by mutual consent truly reflects the reality of what has occurred.

Thus, a clause in your contract to the effect that your employment will 'automatically terminate', if, for example, you fail to return to work on the due date after a period of leave, is likely to be regarded as an invalid attempt to 'contract out' of modern job security laws.

Retractions

Occasionally, courts and tribunals take the view that a dismissal or resignation given in the heat of the moment can be withdrawn. It is fair to say that, in so doing, they are applying sensible principles of good industrial relations rather than the strict law of contract.

In any event, you would do well to strive to avoid the uncertainty of a dispute about the legal effect of words said at a time when tempers flare. This means not only avoiding the use of words which might amount to a resignation on your part, but also checking whether words that apparently mean that your job has ended were actually intended to have that effect.

Fixed-term contracts

If your employer fails to renew a fixed-term contract, you are deemed to have been dismissed in law. On the other hand, where a contract for a specific purpose comes to an end, there is no dismissal.

The dividing line between the two forms of agreement is often fine. Typical is the case of *Wiltshire County Council v NATFHE and Guy* (1980). Ms Guy worked as a part-time teacher from 1969 to 1977. She entered into a fresh contract each academic year. Her appointment was not renewed in 1977–78.

The Court of Appeal held that there had been a dismissal. The employee worked under a contract for a fixed, specified period from the start of the autumn term to the last day of the summer term. The argument that she was employed for the specific purpose of teaching students, and therefore not eligible for dismissal rights, was rejected.

Subsequent agreements

What happens if, while you are under notice of dismissal, you wish to leave your job before the notice expires in order to work elsewhere?

If your employer agrees to your early departure, you will still be regarded as dismissed in law if the agreement is simply, in effect, to bring forward your dismissal date or if it is agreed that you need not actually work during the remainder of your notice period. On the other hand, if the reality is that you have mutually agreed to the ending of the contract, then you will not be entitled to dismissal rights.

While courts and tribunals will again be reluctant to conclude that you have forfeited your entitlements, it makes sense to ensure that there is no question of your employer being able to argue later that there was no dismissal, if that does not suit you. It is a good idea to record the position specifically in a letter or memo.

If your employer does not agree to your leaving during the notice period, you are entitled under the Consolidation Act to give counter-notice. This may be verbal and, strangely, the Act does not specify how long your notice should be.

16.3 What is the date of dismissal?

Even if it is clear that you have been dismissed, the precise date when your employment comes to an end may be unclear. Yet you are likely to need to know the exact date when your job terminates for several reasons, such as to ascertain:

1. whether you have the relevant period of continuous employment to qualify for various statutory entitlements like redundancy pay and unfair dismissal rights;
2. the amount of any redundancy payment or unfair dismissal 'basic award' to which you may be entitled;
3. from when your time begins to run for presenting any complaint to an industrial tribunal;
4. whether, at the date of termination, you were eligible for various rights, for instance in view of your age or location overseas.

The employment legislation lays down a series of rules as regards the date of dismissal. Basically, that date is:

(a) where your contract is terminated by notice, whether given by yourself or by your employer, the date on which that notice expires;
(b) where the contract is not terminated by notice, the date on which its termination takes effect;
(c) where there is a fixed-term contract, the date on which that term expires.

There are a number of additional provisions to cater for special circumstances. For example, a failure to allow a woman employee to return to work after maternity leave is treated as a dismissal, with the termination date being the date notified by her as the date of return.

Ambiguous dismissal letters
Interpreting the facts correctly often becomes even harder because

of the vague way in which many dismissals are implemented. A typical example occurred in *Adams v G K N Sankey Ltd* (1980). A letter written in November 1979 said: 'You are given twelve weeks' notice of dismissal from this company with effect from 5.11.79. You will not be expected to work out your notice but will receive money in lieu of notice . . .' The payment was made without deduction of tax, and pension rights were treated as ending on 5 November 1979.

Nevertheless, the Employment Appeal Tribunal held that the termination date occurred only upon expiry of the 12-week notice period. This was a case of an employee being sent home on paid leave during his notice. All that happened was that the right to require his actual service was waived.

In interpreting a vague letter, a tribunal should be guided by:

1. the way in which an ordinary, reasonable employee would understand the words used;
2. the facts known to the employee at the date he received the letter;
3. the principle of interpreting ambiguous words against the person who used them, so as not to encourage employers to mislead by deliberate vagueness.

Shortening the notice period

As we saw earlier, either you or your employer may wish to shorten the notice period. If your company attempts to do so, tribunals will again construe any ambiguity in your favour, if there is a risk that you might be disadvantaged by what your employer purports to have done.

Unfortunately, there are limits to the extent to which tribunals can lean in your favour in such a case. In *Stapp v Shaftesbury Society* (1982), the employer brought the job to a premature end before the expiry of the one month's notice period originally specified. The effect was to bar the luckless employee from unfair dismissal rights, even though he would have had sufficient continuous employment to found a claim had the original termination date stood.

The Court of Appeal did not consider that the second notice was invalid because it amounted to a means of depriving the employee of his statutory rights. However, the second notice was clearly given in breach of contract and it was indicated that in any subsequent wrongful dismissal action, damages might include a sum for the loss of the right to claim unfair dismissal to which the employee would have been entitled had the contract been honoured.

Statutory postponement

If you are not given sufficient notice in accordance with your contract, the Consolidation Act provides that the termination date for certain purposes will be when either:

1. the actual notice given expires; or
2. the minimum *statutory* notice period (see Chapter 6) would have expired;

whichever is the later.

It is important to appreciate that the *contractual* notice period is not added to your period of service. This may be bad news if you do not have sufficient continuous service to qualify for rights if only the statutory period is added, although you would have had sufficient service if the longer notice period to which you are entitled under your contract were added.

If you have been validly dismissed for gross misconduct, you cannot add the statutory minimum notice period to your period of service. Nor does the statutory postponement apply for the purpose of ascertaining whether you have made a complaint to an industrial tribunal within the requisite time limit.

Internal appeals

If you appeal against your dismissal, and your appeal is rejected, you may wonder whether your job legally came to an end at the time of your original dismissal or when the appeal was eventually turned down.

The answer will depend upon how the appeals procedure is framed. If payment of your salary continues until the date of final rejection, that date is likely to be the termination date. In most cases, however, the original date of dismissal will be the important date. This means that, if you do pursue an appeal, you should not overlook any relevant time limits for pursuing your statutory rights. If you do, you risk achieving the worst of both worlds by finding that the appeals procedure becomes protracted, that you are not ultimately allowed to resume your job and that you have missed the chance to complain to an industrial tribunal about your treatment.

Chapter 17

Valuing Your Statutory Rights

17.1 What is your job worth?

If your job is at risk, you should be aware of the hard cash value of your legal rights. Quite apart from potentially valuable entitlements under your contract, which are discussed in Chapter 18, you may be eligible to claim a redundancy payment and/or that your dismissal is unfair. The main qualifying conditions are outlined in Chapter 20.

The value of unfair dismissal rights is not purely financial. If a tribunal holds your dismissal to be unfair, it must consider which remedy to grant. The possibilities are:

1. reinstatement, ie an order that you shall be treated in every respect as if you had not been dismissed; or
2. re-engagement, ie re-employment on terms which are not identical to those enjoyed at the date of your dismissal; or
3. compensation.

The tribunal must consider the remedies in that order. Nevertheless, unfairly dismissed employees are only awarded re-employment in a very small minority of cases. In particular, business executives hardly ever regain their jobs. This is presumably because it is seldom possible to heal the breach that is usually created by fighting a legal battle.

Even if reinstatement or re-engagement is ordered, an employer cannot at the end of the day be forced to take you back. The ultimate sanction is financial: an additional award of compensation.

Knowing what your rights may be worth in money terms will help you not only to decide whether or not to take legal action, if necessary, to recover the sums due to you, but also to assess the reasonableness of any 'termination package deal' offered to you and generally to plan ahead for the future.

17.2 Redundancy payments

The amount of a statutory redundancy payment is calculated as follows:

1. for each year of employment between the ages of 18 and 21 – half a week's pay;
2. for each year of employment between the ages of 22 and 40 – one week's pay;
3. for each year of employment between the ages of 41 and 65 – one and a half week's pay;
4. employment for longer than 20 years is not taken into account;
5. the maximum amount of a week's pay taken into account with effect from 1 April 1990 is £184 per week, but that figure is reviewed from time to time. The amount currently applicable should be checked with the Department of Employment;
6. in the year before the employee's 65th birthday, various provisions scale down the payment on a monthly basis, ie the amount is reduced by one twelfth for each month by which his or her age approaches 65;
7. no deduction is made for tax.

The relevant date for calculating your pay is normally the date on which your job would have terminated had proper notice been given under the Consolidation Act, whether or not such notice was in fact given. In effect, therefore, the redundancy payment is based on final earnings. A week's pay is calculated in accordance with a series of statutory rules. Most business executives will find the arbitrary cut-off point of £184 means that state redundancy pay is worth rather less than they might have hoped or expected.

Your employer must give you a written statement when making a redundancy payment, showing how the amount is calculated, unless the amount of payment has already been fixed by the decision of an industrial tribunal.

17.3 Unfair dismissal basic award

The concept of the basic award in unfair dismissal is akin to that of the redundancy payment, ie it reflects loss of job security. It is calculated in almost exactly the same way. However, deductions may be made from it if:

1. your conduct was such that it would be just and equitable to make a deduction;
2. it was just and equitable to make a deduction because you unreasonably refused an offer of reinstatement;
3. your dismissal date fell after your 64th birthday, in which case the award is reduced on a sliding scale.

Furthermore, a statutory redundancy payment will be offset against the basic award.

17.4 The compensatory award

If you are entitled to compensation for unfair dismissal, you will usually receive a compensatory award as well as a basic award. The compensatory award is intended to reimburse you for financial loss resulting from the unfair dismissal. The award will be the amount that the tribunal considers just and equitable in all the circumstances. It will cover any expenses reasonably incurred and any loss of benefit which you might reasonably be expected to have had but for the dismissal. Legal costs for assistance with an unfair dismissal claim are not reimbursed.

The onus is upon you to show that you have suffered loss and, if you have suffered no loss because your job would have ended in any event, there will be a nil award.

Compensation may be limited if a fair dismissal would, or might, have been possible in the near future, ie where the unfairness lay primarily in accelerating your dismissal.

In *Winterhalter Gastronom Ltd v Webb* (1973), an employee, dismissed unfairly for incompetence because a fair period to improve was not allowed, nevertheless saw his compensation halved by the Employment Appeal Tribunal, who concluded that:

> His chances of improving sufficiently to hold down his job were poor and . . . only a modest sum can be fairly attributed to the loss of this chance.

This principle might not be restricted to cases of misconduct or lack of capability. For example, if you are unfairly made redundant because consideration was not given to offering you another job, your compensation might be discounted to take account of the fact that, had proper consideration been given, you might still not have been offered that job.

In assessing compensation, a tribunal has wide discretion. The Employment Appeal Tribunal has expressed the view that any other approach would tend to defeat the system's objectives of speed, informality and accessibility. It is accepted that this:

> may mean that sometimes an employee will get a bit less than he might have expected; it may mean that sometimes an employer will have to pay a little more than he had expected.

17.5 Quantifying the compensatory award

Unfortunately, but perhaps inevitably, the calculation of the compensatory award is highly speculative. Making an advance estimate of its amount in a particular case is fraught with danger.

Above all, you should be aware of an extremely important ceiling on the compensatory award. With effect from 1 April 1990, the maximum award is £8,925; that limit is reviewed from time to time.

The effect of this regrettable and wholly arbitrary restriction is that, for a senior executive, an unfair dismissal claim may provide only a very limited redress for the losses resulting from the unjust ending of employment.

Earnings during the notice period

If you are dismissed with pay in lieu of notice, or without notice, and you obtain new employment during the notice period, you are bound to bring into account those earnings.

Manner of dismissal

If you suffer loss as a result of the manner of an unfair dismissal, for example because you lose the chance of another job when your prospective employer learns that you have been sacked, you will be compensated for that loss. In practice, you will seldom find it easy to show that you have suffered in that way and, in particular, you are not entitled to compensation to reflect the emotional distress than an unjust dismissal may well cause both you and your family.

Loss to date of hearing

You will normally be able to claim the amount (net of tax and National Insurance) that you would have earned between the date of dismissal and the date of the industrial tribunal hearing. From this will be deducted the amount that you have earned if you have found another job. If you begin new employment before the hearing, that will not operate as a 'cut-off' date. Instead, the earnings in your new job will usually be set off against what you have lost.

Sickness benefits received prior to the hearing need only be brought into account where your salary would have been reduced on account of ill health. Social security benefits will be set off against your loss; the relevant rules are contained in detailed regulations.

The tribunal must specify various elements in its award of compensation if you have received certain state benefits. First, the total monetary award will be calculated. Second, the amount of the compensaton, and the period covered by it, from the dismissal date to the date of the hearing, will be identified. This amount is called 'the prescribed element'. Finally, the amount by which the total award exceeds the prescribed element must also be specified.

The prescribed element is, in effect, frozen for the time being and should not be paid by the employer. The Department of Employment may serve a recoupment notice on the employer within 21 days of the end of the hearing, or within nine days after the decision is sent to the parties (21 days if the judgment has been reserved). Your former employer should pay the amount so claimed by the Department in respect of social security benefits that you have received. Any part of the prescribed element remaining should then be paid by you.

These rules do not bite where a claim is settled, thus providing an additional incentive to both sides to reach a private agreement.

Future loss

The onus is on you to show that you will suffer loss after the hearing date as a result of being treated unjustly. If you have found work elsewhere at a lower salary before the hearing, the tribunal will have to project your loss forward for whatever period it considers appropriate.

If you are still out of work, the tribunal has to gaze into its crystal ball. In effect, it will try to guess how long you will be out of work. Your age and skills, as well as the local employment situation, will usually be highly relevant, but again the tribunal's discretion is very wide indeed.

Fringe benefits

The tribunal will generally compensate you for lost fringe benefits, although putting a figure upon them is often another exercise in guesstimation.

Quantifying the value of your lost pension rights is a particularly difficult task. The Government Actuary's Department prepared a document in 1980 which sets out a suggested basis for making the calculation and this was supplemented ten years later by recommendations from a committee of industrial tribunal chairmen. While an industrial tribunal may err if it misinterprets these guidelines, the Employment Appeal Tribunal has emphasised that, for all the potential complexity, the assessment of compensation is inevitably a rough-and-ready exercise.

Loss of employment protection rights

You will generally be awarded a sum in respect of your lost industrial rights, ie because you have to requalify for the right not to be unfairly dismissed. In 1986, the Employment Appeal Tribunal suggested that the going rate under this heading was £100. Nowadays a slightly higher figure is apt to be awarded.

Expenses

You may be entitled to compensation in respect of certain expenses incurred, for instance in seeking new employment. Removal expenses might be recoverable if you have to leave the district in order to improve your employment prospects. It is even possible that if you decide to set up your own business, you may be able to claim for the initial costs of this.

17.6 Deductions

Contributory fault

If a tribunal decides that, although your dismissal was unfair, you were partly to blame, it will reduce your compensation by the amount it considers just and equitable. This may apply even in a case of constructive dismissal.

Once again, the tribunal has a very wide discretion. It is even possible, in extreme circumstances, for contributory fault to be assessed at 100 per cent, thus resulting in a nil compensation award.

The Employment Appeal Tribunal has said that the weight to be given to an employee's conduct ought to be decided 'in a broad, common sense manner'. Bloody-mindedness may sometimes amount to contributory fault, as may any particularly unreasonable behaviour.

Mitigation of loss

The compensatory award may be reduced if you have failed to mitigate your loss. This concept also applies in breach-of-contract claims, and is further discussed in Chapter 18. Similar principles apply in unfair dismissal cases.

Ex gratia payments

Quantifying compensation may be complicated if an *ex gratia* payment has been made to you.

For example, an *ex gratia* payment is not automatically treated as meeting any liability stemming from the basic award. If it was clearly intended that the *ex gratia* sum should include an element to cover the basic award, it will be set off against that award, but not otherwise. If a general payment is made, the tribunal will have to interpret whether it does actually cover both basic and compensatory awards.

What happens if you are paid an *ex gratia* sum which exceeds the current maximum compensatory award? Are you able to claim any additional compensation if you have been unfairly dismissed? The answer is sometimes yes. The *ex gratia* payment should be deducted from the total gross award, which may far exceed the meagre statutory limit, before that limit is applied. Thus, if the total award is large enough (say, reflecting three years' employment and loss of salary and contract benefits for that length of time), an *ex gratia* payment will not reduce your former employer's legal liability towards you at all.

Furthermore, any reduction in respect of contributory fault should only be made after the *ex gratia* payment has been subtracted from the total gross award. This is another reason why a well-advised employer who offers you an *ex gratia* payment when your job comes to an end is likely to insist that you are effectively prevented in law from making any further claim against him (see Chapter 19).

Chapter 18

What is Your Contract Worth?

18.1 Wrongful dismissal

If your employment contract is broken and you suffer loss as a result, you will probably wish to seek compensation. In the case of a small pay cut, for example, we have seen that it is sometimes safer to sue for the amount that you have lost, rather than give up your job. Where a more serious breach of contract occurs, or you are sacked, you will need to consider whether or not to claim that you have been wrongfully dismissed.

One point to clear up immediately is the widespread confusion between wrongful dismissal and unfair dismissal. They are two distinct legal concepts.

A wrongful dismissal may be fair. On the other hand, an unfair dismissal may not be wrongful. The rules and procedures in the two actions are very different. The right not to be unfairly dismissed is relatively modern and based upon statute; if you are unfairly dismissed, you may complain to an industrial tribunal. A wrongful dismissal claim is a common law action for damages for breach of contract.

One of the unsatisfactory features of employment law over the past couple of decades has been the rule that a wrongful dismissal claim must be brought in either the County Court or the High Court. Complex cases, or those where the sum at stake is above a specified limit, have been the sole province of the High Court. Unfortunately proceedings in the civil courts tend to be slower, more expensive and more formal than those in the industrial tribunal. Yet the cap on the compensatory award for unfair dismissal discussed in Chapter 17 meant that a significant number of executives had little option but to fight through the thickets of civil court procedure.

The scene was complicated by the introduction of the Wages Act 1986. The key principle of the Act is that an employer should not make a deduction from the wages of a worker without that worker's written consent. Under the Act, a worker may present a complaint about an unlawful deduction from his wages to an industrial tribunal. As the Act became more widely known, people began to bring in the industrial tribunal claims which were, in effect, wrongful dismissal claims in disguise – typically, claims in respect of non-payment of notice monies. Confusion increased when different industrial tribunals and different divisions of the Employment Appeal Tribunal disagreed about whether it was legitimate under the Act to pursue such claims. It may have been no coincidence that the Government announced in March 1990 that industrial tribunals were to be given the power to hear claims for damages in respect of breaches of employment contract.

This is a welcome and long overdue development but at the time of writing the detailed regulations bringing it into force have yet to be published. Even when the new system is operational, it will be subject to important conditions. First, the claim must arise or be outstanding on the termination of the employee's employment. Second, it must arise in circumstances which also give rise to proceedings already or simultaneously brought before an industrial tribunal.

The civil courts will not be deprived by this measure of jurisdiction for breach of employment contract claims. Unless some specific provision is made limiting the power of a tribunal to hear claims involving large sums or very complex issues, it will be for the employee to choose the forum in which he will pursue his claim. Only time will tell whether the requirement that 'other proceedings' must be brought will lead to an increase in more or less spurious statute-based complaints, for instance in respect of unfair dismissal.

There are a variety of reasons why, despite this new move, you may still wish (or be obliged) to bring a wrongful dismissal claim in the civil courts, for example:

1. where you have insufficient service to quality for unfair dismissal rights;
2. where you are ineligible on other grounds to claim unfair dismissal, perhaps because you are past normal retiring age or fall within an excluded category of employment;
3. where you have missed the time limit for presenting an unfair dismissal application (the normal limitation period for bringing an action for breach of contract in the civil courts is six

years, rather than the strict three-month time limit for pursuing an unfair dismissal claim);
4. where your dismissal, although wrongful, was plainly fair, such as a dismissal for genuine and inevitable redundancy, but with inadequate notice;
5. where you stand to gain very much more from a successful action for wrongful dismissal than you would from proceeding before an industrial tribunal, bearing in mind the ceiling on unfair dismissal compensation and the potential value of your contract if your notice entitlement is lengthy.

Occasionally, it is both possible and desirable to launch claims in respect of both unfair dismissal and wrongful dismissal (see below).

What do you stand to gain in a wrongful dismissal case? The basic rule of the common law is that:

> where a party sustains a loss by reason of a breach of contract, he is, so far as money can do it, to be placed in the same situation with respect to damages, as if the contract had been performed.

These words, uttered by Baron Parke in an 1848 case, still hold good today. The crux is that the amount of damages obtainable will, *prima facie*, be the total of the salary and fringe benefits to which you would have been entitled between the time of the job actually ending and the time at which the contract could lawfully have been ended by due notice.

18.2 Salary during the notice period

The major part of your claim will usually be your right to salary during the notice period. This is where hard bargaining at the time that you negotiated your service contract could pay off handsomely.

For example, if you have been employed for four years and earn a basic salary of £40,000, one hardly need emphasise the difference between the value of your rights if you are eligible just for the statutory minimum of four weeks' notice and the scale of your claim if you are on, say, a three-year rolling contract. The length of your notice period will also govern the worth of your fringe benefits in the event of a wrongful dismissal.

Although a breach of contract claim is based upon common law rights, remember that the Consolidation Act entitles you to minimum pay during your statutory notice period. Even if you do not work some or all of your normal hours during that period, you should still be paid for them if you are:

1. ready and willing to work, but given no work;
2. incapable of work through sickness or injury;
3. taking your lawful holidays.

18.3 Motor car

If you are only allowed to use your 'company car' in connection with your job, you will probably not be entitled to compensation for loss of the right to use it during your notice period if you are not being asked to work.

More often, an executive's contract entitles him to private use of his car. This, after all, is one of the commonest fringe benefits. Nevertheless, you should check the exact scope of your rights under the contract. Are you, for instance, due to be reimbursed in respect of all or part of the running expenses?

It is rare for a dispute about the value of an executive's car to reach the courts. An illuminating exception to this general rule occurred in *Shove v Downs Surgical plc* (1984). Mr Shove joined the company in 1937 and eventually became chairman and managing director. In July 1982, he fell ill and the following month his fellow directors decided in his absence to sack him. He was not given the 30 months' notice provided for by his contract.

Among other things, the company argued that he had no right to use the car for his private purposes. The High Court disagreed. Had that been so, it would not have been necessary for his contract to include a statement that, 'the Company will bear the entire cost of servicing, repairing, maintaining, taxing and insuring the said motor car'. Furthermore, Mr Shove was entitled to charge the company for private petrol. The contract made no mention of this, but there was evidence that, in practice, he had been allowed to have petrol for private use.

The company claimed that Mr Shove's financial loss as a result of being deprived of private use of the car should be calculated by referring to the tax charge on it. Again, the judge rejected this argument. Nor would he accept that he should work out the sum due by looking at the cost of providing a type of car which Mr Shove 'might reasonably be expected to acquire in his present circumstances'. Mr Shove was entitled under his contract to the benefit of a Daimler throughout his notice period and that is what he was compensated for.

There are several different ways in which the loss can be assessed. One way would be to take the cost of buying a car of the same age and then trying to quantify the cost of running it throughout the notice period. Another method would be to look at the Automobile Association's figures on the cost of running a motor car of that engine capacity or at the cost of hiring such a car.

18.4 Pension rights

Your pension is valuable. If you are wrongfully dismissed, the cost in terms of pension benefits alone is likely to be heavy. Saying that is, unfortunately, much easier than calculating in hard cash terms exactly what you have lost.

In unfair dismissal cases, it is understandable that industrial tribunals tend to shrink away from complex arithmetic. As we have seen, even though the Government Actuary's Department's guidelines are helpful, a rough-and-ready approach is perhaps inevitable.

In a wrongful dismissal case, where there is no equivalent to the statutory ceiling on the amount of compensation that may be awarded, it will often be worth taking the trouble to investigate the pension position in much more depth.

Once more, there are a number of different methods of calculating the loss. If it is likely to be sizeable, it might be a good idea to hire a consultancy actuary to analyse the scheme involved and to pinpoint the relevant facts. Pensions are often structured in a complex way and there may be plenty of material for an ingenious expert to get his teeth into. With careful thought and the application of ruthless logic, it may be possible to establish a much larger claim than you would have expected. If so, your investment in professional help will have been amply justified.

18.5 Commission and bonuses

If you have a contractual right to commission or a bonus, you are entitled to be compensated for what you have lost as a result of a wrongful dismissal.

This is so even though, inevitably, the amount that you might earn is variable. If the matter ever came to court, the judge would estimate the amount that you would have earned, in the light of the evidence before him concerning the nature of your job.

Similar principles apply in the case of bonuses, which often involve an element of profit sharing. The first step is to look at the contract to see whether there is any discretion with regard to payment that is made. If the company has the right to decide whether or not to award a bonus, you will not be entitled to compensation for its loss, unless the bonus has been declared by the date of your dismissal.

If the contract makes it clear that you will receive a bonus, without specifying a fixed sum, your entitlement is probably to a figure that is reasonable, taking into account sums received in previous years.

18.6 Other benefits

As we saw in Chapter 4, your contract may cater for a wide variety of perks, such as:

1. life assurance;
2. private health care;
3. free or subsidised accommodation;
4. loans on favourable terms;
5. free or subsidised meals;
6. home telephone charges;
7. rights under share incentive schemes;
8. professional subscriptions.

The list is almost endless. You should not underestimate the importance of these rights when working out the value of your contract. For example, in the Shove case, the sum awarded by the High Court under the first two headings in the above list alone amounted to £7300: not a trifling amount.

18.7 Hurt feelings

To be sacked on the spot, or with inadequate notice, is likely to distress even the most resilient of businessmen. No one who has undergone the traumatic and humiliating experience of being bundled unceremoniously out of a senior position will deny that. Grossly unfair treatment could affect your physical and mental well-being, as well as that of members of your close family.

Regrettably, a House of Lords decision in the early years of this century made it clear that wrongful dismissal compensation will not cover either:

1. injury to personal feelings; or

2. loss suffered because the dismissal makes it more difficult for you to find another job.

A few exceptions to this harsh rule have emerged over the years. A person involved in the entertainment industry, such as an actor, might be able to claim if his contract clearly envisaged that publicity would enhance his reputation. Furthermore, in 1975 an executive who suffered emotional distress after being demoted was awarded £500 compensation.

The current trend, however, is for the old orthodoxy to be re-asserted. Thus, in the Shove case, even though the judge accepted that Mr Shove had suffered distress as a result of being so deplorably treated, no damages were awarded because of that.

This seems unfair. One can claim compensation for the dismaying experience of a spoilt holiday: it is strange that the same principle does not apply to the breaking of obligations under employment contracts. Perhaps one day some brave soul will make a long legal journey to the House of Lords and persuade them to change their minds.

18.8 Deductions

Taxation

Damages for breach of contract should put you as nearly as possible in the position that you would have occupied had your contract been performed properly – but no better. Because you would have received your pay and benefits net of tax if you had worked, your damages must take tax into account.

Complications arise if one tries to tie in this principle with the favourable tax treatment of 'golden handshakes', discussed in more detail in Chapter 19. Over the years, the courts have adopted varying approaches.

One possibility is to ignore the part of the award of damages which exceeds the amount exempt from tax under the 'golden handshake' rules, for instance by expressing the exempt amount (currently £30,000) as an annual income over the unexpired period of the contract, estimating what the tax would be on that imaginary income and deducting that tax from the total compensation.

This artificial exercise was not repeated in the Shove case. The High Court sought to make the final damages reflect Mr Shove's actual loss. The chosen method was to calculate his net loss, taking into account that he would have paid income tax on earnings, then adding back 'golden handshake' tax so that he would be left with the net amount after the Revenue had collected tax on the damages.

There are several obvious difficulties:
1. one cannot guess how tax rates, personal allowances and bands of income for higher rates are going to change in future tax years;
2. the amount of your personal allowances may change for various reasons;
3. you may have other income, pushing your total income into higher-rate bands;
4. if you worked abroad, any tax relief that might be associated with your periods overseas ought to be considered.

Mitigation of loss
You are obliged to keep your losses to a minimum. The basic legal principles are:
1. you cannot recover loss that you could have avoided suffering by taking reasonable steps;
2. if you in fact avoid or reduce your loss, you cannot recover the amount so saved, even if the steps that you took were more than could reasonably have been expected;
3. you may recover loss or expense incurred in taking reasonable steps to mitigate your loss.

If you are wrongfully dismissed, you should therefore seek alternative employment at the earliest opportunity. Wages that you earn or could reasonably have earned during your notice period will be taken into account when assessing compensation.

Whether or not you can reasonably be expected to take a job of a different kind or at a lower rate of pay will depend upon the circumstances. The rules are not rigid. If you occupied a senior position, you may not be under an immediate duty to accept an alternative job of an inferior status. If so, you may look for work of the same status, remunerated at the same level, for a reasonable time, without having your compensation reduced as a result.

As a practical measure, keep a full record of all jobs that you apply for and the responses that you receive to show that you have not simply sat back and waited for the money to roll in.

State benefits
If you receive state benefits, such as unemployment benefit, during your notice period, they will be taken into account in calculating the extent of your claim. This is another example of the way in which damages are intended to reflect only what you have really lost.

Accelerated payment

It takes some time for a breach of contract claim to reach a trial. Occasionally, however, a compensation award will be made and become payable before the expiry of the notice period. In such circumstances, the courts will usually make a deduction because you are receiving early payment. In the Shove case, the compensation was reduced for this reason by 7 per cent, a figure which had been agreed between the parties.

In the context of pre-trial negotiations, and discussions about a termination package (see Chapter 19), you may also find that the company will insist that the value of your claim should be reduced to take account of this factor. This is often a logical argument and the real issue may be the amount of the deduction that should be made.

Contributory fault

One of the attractions of a breach of contract claim is that there is no provision for contributory fault. If you have been guilty of a fundamental breach of your obligations under the contract, you will, of course, have been lawfully dismissed and therefore entitled to no compensation. Thus, wrongful dismissal sometimes proves to be 'all or nothing' litigation.

18.9 Overlap with unfair dismissal

Although there are a number of points of difference, some of them highly significant, between the calculation of compensation for unfair dismissal and for wrongful dismissal, there is nonetheless often a degree of overlap.

While you are not entitled to recover twice the same amount of loss, it is conceivable that you might be eligible for full compensation in respect of both claims. This might happen, for instance, if you were unfairly dismissed without notice at the age of 60, when you had no prospect of finding another job before an expected retirement age of 65. If your notice period was 12 months, you might obtain damages to cover that period and yet still be asking an industrial tribunal to reimburse you to the extent of the maximum compensatory award in respect of your anticipated future loss, together with payment to you of the basic award.

A number of important tactical questions may need to be answered. For example, would it be prudent to ask the tribunal to postpone hearing your unfair dismissal claim pending the outcome of the breach of contract case? This might be sensible if you were advised that your claim would be better presented in the formal atmosphere of the civil courts, or that your wrongful dismissal claim is so much more substantial that it will lead almost inevitably to a settlement of the lesser, unfair dismissal claim.

It is worth bearing in mind, too, that a judgment in the industrial tribunal may bind the High Court and vice versa. In which forum is your version of events most likely to be accepted? Expert advice on such matters is indispensable.

Chapter 19

Termination Package Deals

19.1 The gentle art of compromise

Inevitably, a book such as this harps on the pitfalls faced by executives. You may easily gain the impression that only cynics survive and that every businessman needs a tame lawyer at his elbow when dealing with his own boss.

The good news is that, even in the minority of cases where the only solution is to leave your job and try your luck elsewhere, it is unusual for a dispute to arise that is so serious that you finish up in front of a judge or an industrial tribunal. Whether you are leaving on a more or less amicable basis, perhaps just a luckless victim of business recession or a change in management style following a takeover, or in an atmosphere of mutual recrimination, it is usually possible sooner or later to strike a deal with the company which satisfies both sides.

If tempers have flared, and especially if you have been badly treated by your employer, the urge to retaliate with every means at your disposal will be enormous. Firing off a writ or an unfair dismissal application may make you feel better for a little while, but you should think carefully before launching yourself into a full-scale battle. Although there are times when pursuing litigation is tactically the right thing to do, and others when there is simply no realistic alternative, you need to be conscious of the possible drawbacks.

For example, how will suing your former employer affect your chances of finding another job? However unjust it might be, there are many companies which will be inclined to think twice about recruiting someone who is engaged in a bitter fight with his old firm. If you retain real career ambitions, this is a harsh truth which you cannot entirely ignore, even if in the end you decide that you must not abandon your legal rights of redress.

The risks of a court case also have to be in the forefront of your mind. Most lawyers will tell you that 'cast iron' prospects of success are much less common than their clients are apt to believe. What seems plain maltreatment at the time could look rather different in the quiet surroundings of a tribunal or courtroom months or years later. Indulging in litigation may mean that you have to expend substantial sums of money and wait a long time before achieving victory; to lose could prove very costly. You have to take account of the worry to your family and yourself as well as the advice that you receive on the merits of your claims.

Any or all of these factors may encourage you to seek to negotiate a settlement which entitles you to speedy payment of a lump sum and perhaps other benefits, even if the value of the total package is less than the amount that you might theoretically win if you sued and all went well.

Similarly, your employer, whether out of a genuine spirit of goodwill, a hard-headed assessment of the damage that a court case might do or a combination of the two, may decide that the best course is to seek an amicable parting of the ways. Frequently, senior executives are offered a termination package deal at the time when they are first told that it is likely or unavoidable that their job will come to an end.

Don't become despondent just because it seems that your employer is keen to drive a hard bargain. Above all, remember that both parties are not irrevocably committed to litigation just because legal proceedings are issued. Wrongful dismissal actions seldom reach a full trial in the High Court and about 70 per cent of all unfair dismissal claims are settled or withdrawn without the need for a hearing. It is plain that, in the long run, the gentle art of compromise has much to recommend it.

19.2 Negotiating techniques

There are many different approaches to the negotiation of termination package deals. Some advisers suggest that you look to past precedents within the company; others recommend that you gear your expectations to the financial sum that you expect to require in order to exist in reasonable comfort until another job comes along; others simply suggest that you look for payment of a year's full salary.

From a legal point of view, a useful rule of thumb is that the maximum of a dismissed executive's legal claims is likely to be the total of:

1. statutory redundancy pay (or an unfair dismissal basic award);
2. the current maximum unfair dismissal compensatory award; and
3. the total value of his contractual rights during his notice period.

Time and again this simple formula proves to be a constructive starting point for detailed discussion. Naturally, it has limitations. For instance, if the dismissal was plainly fair or the executive lacks sufficient service to claim unfair dismissal, the first two elements may be irrelevant. But this approach avoids undervaluing your claims. Indeed, you will probably find it difficult to construct a logical argument to the effect that you are legally entitled to a higher sum than can be arrived at by applying the above calculation.

How you conduct negotiations from there is largely a question of individual judgment supported by sound professional advice. You need to exploit not only your commercial acumen, but also your personal knowledge of the people with whom you are dealing. Do they really mean it when they say that a proposal is 'not negotiable' or conditional upon your acceptance within a very strict time limit? Are these men who have to be pushed every inch of the way? Is the first offer that they make simply an opening shot?

Some employers are unwilling to pay the whole settlement sum 'upfront'. They may insist on payment by instalments, possibly spread throughout the whole of your notice period. Even more worryingly, continued payment of the instalments may be conditional upon your observing a variety of undertakings – typically including restrictions on competing activities. You need to think long and hard before agreeing to such 'strings'. And if you do agree to them, but later have second thoughts, seek expert advice before doing anything which might expose you to legal action, or to the risk that the instalment payments will be stopped. In particular, try to avoid agreeing to any deal which allows your employer to claw back moneys already paid, if you (perhaps unwittingly) transgress the terms of the deal.

At all times, you need to remain aware of the risk factors mentioned in the previous section. There may also be a wide variety of specific points which influence your thinking. If you have another lucrative position lined up, that will be a good reason to press for an early resolution if you fear that once your ex-employer learns of it, he might be much less inclined to generosity. While it is only sensible to acknowledge that the company will have greater resources and possibly less to lose than yourself, your hand could be strengthened if you are confident that messy litigation is the last thing that management wants because, for example, a merger is on the horizon or the publicity of a court case is likely to upset customers.

Although the adrenalin may flow, you owe it to yourself not to become carried away. Over the years, a few huge, widely reported pay-offs have given rise to the impression among more gullible members of the newspaper-reading public that six-figure golden handshakes are the norm for the departing business executive. Do not be deceived into throwing away a decent offer in pursuit of pie in the sky.

19.3 Tax implications of termination payments

Before you fix on a settlement figure, you need to consider how much tax you will have to pay on any agreed sum and whether the tax burden can somehow be reduced. As ever, there is much to be gained from seeking expert advice at an early stage, especially since tax law changes at least as rapidly as employment law and your personal circumstances may also affect the view that you ought to take. Only a brief outline of the main points which currently affect business executives can be given here.

Golden handshakes
The basic rule is that termination payments are generally regarded by the Inland Revenue as fully taxable pay, unless they are:

1. gifts expressing personal regard for the employee's qualities, in the case of a parting or by mutual consent; or
2. compensation for loss of office, in the case of dismissal or forced resignation.

Suffice it to say here that a payment which is large in relation to salary is unlikely to be viewed as falling within the first category. Usually, you will be more concerned with compensation for loss of office – colloquially known as a golden handshake.

Golden handshakes can be tax efficient. At the time of writing, the whole of a payment by way of compensation for loss of office below £30,000, or the first £30,000 of a larger payment, is tax free. There are anti-avoidance provisions which prevent you gaining from cunning manoeuvres such as arranging for different companies within your employer's group each to contribute a share of the total pay-out; if this is done, all the sums will be aggregated.

'Top-slicing' applies to payments over £30,000. The main points are as follows:

(a) you add different payments in respect of a termination or terminations in the same year and treat them as one;
(b) you deduct the tax-free sum;
(c) you work out how much your tax would be if the non-exempt part of your payment was included in your income. You find the tax due by deducting from that two reliefs:
   - for the part of the payment between the exempt amount and £50,000, first calculate your income tax as if this part were included in your income and then your tax as if it were not; the relief on this part is half the difference;
   - for the part between £50,000 and £75,000, first calculate your tax as if the part between the exempt amount and £75,000 were included in your income, and then your tax as if only the part between the exempt amount and £50,000 were included; the relief on this part is 25 per cent of the difference;
(d) there is no relief on the part of the payment over £75,000.

There are a number of possible tax-saving tactics which you may wish to discuss with your accountant, such as:

- minimising your other taxable income for the year in question;
- leaving soon after the start of the tax year;
- maximising deductions from your other taxable income, for example by making voluntary contributions to an exempt, approved pension scheme.

Pay in lieu of notice
Payments described as being 'in lieu' give rise to much confusion. They can be classified as:

1. genuinely in lieu, ie instead of giving notice; or
2. a wages payment for a notice period which you are not required to work.

In the latter case, the payment is taxable as income. In the former case, it can sometimes be brought within the scope of the rules on payments by way of compensation for loss of office.

If you are told that your employment is to end immediately, but that you will be paid salary for your notice period, that will fall within the former category. However, it would normally be taxable as income in the ordinary way if paid pursuant to a specific clause in your contract. Furthermore, a payment made on the same basis as that in the case of *Adams v G K N Sankey Ltd* mentioned in Chapter 16 would probably also fall within the second category.

19.4   Other parts of the package

Money is not the only thing to think about when you negotiate a termination package deal. Considering what else might be on offer is not only in your interests but may also help bring an overall agreement nearer if your employer is willing to provide non-cash benefits in return, perhaps for a slight reduction in the lump sum that you are looking for.

Take a close look at your pension position. Can your benefits be 'topped up' in a tax-efficient way? Your employer might be willing to purchase an annuity for you to make a one-off lump sum in commutation of your pension rights.

Do not forget the significance of any shares that you hold in the company or any rights that you have under a share incentive scheme. What is to happen and do you have any extra negotiating counters, such as your potential nuisance value as a dissident minority shareholder, which can assist you in persuading the company to be more generous?

There are a number of other practical points to which you may wish to pay attention.

References

It may conceivably help your future career to have a suitably worded reference. Much depends upon you, the company and the job concerned. You have no legal right to insist upon being given a reference; the relevant legal principles are discussed in Chapter 21.

A clause in a severance agreement which merely acknowledges that the company will issue a reference upon being approached by a prospective employer is of little use. You need to know what will be said and a suitable, accurate form of words should be specifically agreed.

Retraining

Occasionally, companies offer departing executives assistance with retraining. This is naturally most relevant in the case of employees whose skills have been overtaken by changing business patterns and the increasing use of new technology and who have fallen victim to redundancy or reorganisation plans.

If this possibility interests you, your main concern should be to ensure that you are given enough information to check that the retraining will be of real practical value. The extent of your employer's duty to pay for it, if the retraining is to be conducted by some outside body, should be made clear.

Out-placement counselling

Everyone knows that, all too often, redundant executives experience difficulty in finding another job. This explains the emergence of out-placement counsellors, consultants who specialise in aiding out-of-work executives to sell themselves effectively in a buyer's market.

Leading counsellors command high fees. Some decline to accept private clients and act only for employers. They can sometimes boast impressive success rates. It may therefore be worth ascertaining whether payment for such services can be included as part of the package.

Consultancy arrangements

If you are not leaving with a sour taste in your mouth, it may be viable for you to enter into an agreement with the company that you will continue to provide it with the benefit of your expertise, pursuant to a consultancy agreement. This may be especially appropriate if you are planning to become self-employed or if retirement age is drawing near. It is less satisfactory if there is a danger of creating a psychological barrier to doing something positive about getting another job.

Needless to say, the arrangement should be recorded in writing. Apart from the question of payment, it will also be especially important to be sure of the precise nature of your commitment in terms of hours to be worked on a weekly or monthly basis.

A word of caution on the subject of tax is also necessary. You need to make sure that, by staying on, you do not cause the Revenue to interpret your lump sum termination package as advance remuneration in disguise and therefore fully taxable. This underlines the need for care when the wording of the total package is discussed.

19.5 'Full and final settlement'

If there is goodwill on both sides, sorting out the precise details of the termination deal may not be too difficult once there is a consensus on the key points of principle.

You will almost inevitably be asked to accept the offer in full and final settlement of all your claims. There is hardly ever a good reason why the deal should not be set out in writing, and this may help to avoid future dispute, but you need to check the proposed wording carefully in conjunction with your advisers.

The first question will usually concern the exact definition of your claims. Does the document refer simply to any rights that you might have against the company that employed you or against every company in the group? What about any claims that you may have against individuals, such as directors of the company? Are you just giving up claims connected with your dismissal or any claim of any sort? If the latter, do you need to negotiate special exceptions, for example in respect of your pension position? What about any claims that may come to light in the future, for instance in relation to products that you may already have bought from the company?

You may be advised that the intended phraseology is appropriate and legally effective. But settling a potential employment dispute tends to involve rather more than just signing a letter prepared by the company or initialling a few sheets of paper which explain the agreed terms.

Employers often insist that departing executives must sign a form supplied by ACAS and make this a fundamental condition of the whole deal. This is because, although a breach of contract claim can be waived by agreeing to a full and final settlement, special rules apply to statutory job security rights such as the unfair dismissal and redundancy payment regimes. The Consolidation Act provides that any clause in an agreement is void in so far as it purports:

1. to exclude or limit the question of any provision of the Act; or
2. to preclude any person from presenting a complaint to an industrial tribunal pursuant to this Act.

The practical effect of this rule is shown by the case of *Council of Engineering Institutions v Maddison* (1976). An employee was made redundant and handed a letter saying that the cheque for £1000 which accompanied it constituted a 'lump sum payment for severance (including redundancy payment), the acceptance of which is final settlement leaving you with no outstanding claim against the Council'.

The Employment Appeal Tribunal was not satisfied that this amounted to a binding agreement, but held that even if it did, it would have been rendered void because it would have been an agreement purporting to preclude the employee from presenting a complaint to a tribunal.

We saw in Chapter 6 that fixed-term contracts offer one, strictly limited, means of contracting out of statutory rights. Even more significant in practice is the rule that settlements of claims under the Act where a conciliation officer from ACAS has 'taken action' are binding.

Impartiality is a vital feature of the conciliation officer's role. He is an independent party through whom you and your employer (or your representatives) can communicate in confidence. He is not a negotiator or a devil's advocate. Consequently, he will not advise on the merits of a settlement offer, although with a view to increasing the likelihood of a deal, he may point out the strengths and weaknesses of each side's arguments. Above all, you should be aware that he is not under an obligation to promote a settlement that is 'fair' or to explain unfair dismissal law to you in great detail. How he performs his function is largely up to him.

When agreement has been reached, it is generally recorded on form COT 3, which is only available from ACAS. If you have already made an application to the tribunal, perhaps to obviate the risk of missing a crucial time limit should negotiations collapse, the detailed terms might, if it is thought appropriate, be set out in a separate document while you withdraw your claim on form COT 4.

Once you have accepted the offer and the position has been suitably documented, you will hardly ever be able to persuade a court or tribunal to upset it unless you can convince them that you were forced to agree as a result of economic duress. Establishing this is extremely difficult; certainly, it is not enough merely to show that you were desperately short of cash.

The conclusion is clear. Do not agree to any deal unless you have assessed in detail all its implications. Once you have agreed, even if the outcome is a compromise that falls short of your original expectations, the sensible thing is to try to stop worrying about what has occurred in the past and to concentrate on the years ahead.

Chapter 20

Going to Law

20.1 The right approach

Ambrose Bierce knew about the pitfalls of the legal process. In *The Devil's Dictionary*, he described litigation as a machine which you go into as a pig and come out of as a sausage. For good measure, he compared a litigant to a person about to give up his skin for the hope of retaining his bones.

There is enough truth in these cynical barbs to justify your thinking twice about becoming directly involved in legal action. A number of potential snags were discussed at the beginning of Chapter 19. No one can doubt that it is far better to aim to prevent job problems arising than to try to cure them by means of a law suit.

Yet it takes two to compromise. Your employer may behave so foolishly or ruthlessly that a sensible settlement of your differences seems impossible. A time may come when you decide, however reluctantly, that you have no alternative but to seek redress by complaining to an industrial tribunal or making a claim through the civil courts.

Litigation is not for the faint-hearted – or the half-hearted. Unless you are prepared to pursue your legal action with a reasonable amount of vigour, you will find that you are wasting both time and money. You need to have the courage of your convictions. Like many a commercial negotiation, litigation sometimes involves an element of brinkmanship; but if you dare not risk your bluff being called, perhaps you should reconsider your plan of campaign.

Above all, effective litigation requires thorough preparation. You should brief your adviser fully and seek his assessment of the pros and cons of your intended course before implementing it. Do not expect a cast-iron guarantee of success. Equally, do not despair just because the path ahead is long and uncertain. Litigation is more like a marathon than a sprint. You need to have staying power.

20.2 Arbitration

Arbitration is a possible alternative to litigation. Arbitration clauses in employment contracts used to be rare. They have become commoner in recent years as business executives and their employers have sought a means of solving disputes without recourse to courts of law. The Government's recent decision to allow industrial tribunals to hear claims relating to breach of the employment contract may, however, bring this trend to a halt.

You cannot contract out of your modern statutory job protection rights. Indeed, the reasonably quick and informal procedure of industrial tribunals is eminently suitable for most cases. But in comparison to proceeding in the civil courts, arbitration offers a number of possible advantages, ie:

1. it is more private than a hearing in the civil courts – the press and public are not entitled to be present;
2. arbitration is quicker than the highly formalised court process;
3. ideally, the chosen arbitrator will be a person with a first-hand grasp of industrial realities, rather than a judge.

Yet arbitration is often not simple, cheap or particularly quick.

That arbitration may often prove less attractive than was originally thought is shown by the case of *Goodman v Winchester and Alton Railway plc* (1984). Mr Goodman's solicitor suggested that his contract should include an arbitration clause because the parties had failed to agree all the terms of his employment before he started work. The idea was that this was a way of ironing out minor disputes, but the clause was worded widely enough to cover a dispute arising out of wrongful termination of the contract.

The contract was for a fixed term of five years. However, after 12 months, Mr Goodman was dismissed. He issued a writ claiming damages for wrongful dismissal. The company, relying on the arbitration clause, argued that the action should be stayed until the case had been heard by an arbitrator. Because this would cause Mr Goodman financial hardship, a High Court judge said that it was wrong to grant a stay.

The Court of Appeal overturned his decision. They accepted that Mr Goodman would suffer financial hardship as a result, but said that they were not in a position to judge whether his dismissal had been justified, so that it could not be said that his difficulties had been caused by the company's conduct. There was no reason to ignore the general presumption that parties who agree to an arbitration clause should be held to their bargain.

20.3 Avoiding dismissal

A business executive who is faced with dismissal usually has to content himself with seeking financial compensation in the form of damages for breach of contract, unfair dismissal compensation or state redundancy pay.

Occasionally, there is a more positive option. In special circumstances, the law of equity may enable you to seek an injunction or declaration, with a view to restraining your employer from carrying out his threat.

A major limitation is that, generally, an injunction will only be granted if the employer was in fact willing to continue with the contract, ie where the real problem was the prospect of unwelcome interference in the contract by a third party. In a 1985 case, however, the High Court granted an injunction against a health authority which was unwilling to continue employing the plaintiff, despite regarding him as a competent worker, because of his personality clash with a more senior colleague. This decision was described as exceptional in *Alexander v Standard Telephones & Cables Ltd* (1990), where the High Court reasserted the traditional principle that the courts should refuse to grant an injunction to restrain a breach of contract which would force an employer to provide work for an employee he does not wish to employ. In the Alexander case, unlike the 1985 case, there was no work for the employee to do and the employers did not have complete confidence in the employee anyway.

So the scope for preserving your job by court order is limited. Even so, an employee with a quick-moving and imaginative lawyer may occasionally be able to launch a surprisingly effective counter-attack when he learns that his job is on the line.

20.4 Are you eligible for rights?

We have already seen that you will not be able to rely upon employment law rights if, in reality, you are not an employee or if your contract is unenforceable, as when it involves an element of illegality.

Where statutory job rights are concerned, you will also be ineligible if:

1. you fall within a category of worker which is specifically excluded from protection; or
2. you are excluded because you do not comply with a specific statutory condition.

The rules vary with the right in question. Thus, Crown servants are not entitled to statutory redundancy payments, but most have the right not to be unfairly dismissed.

One of the most important limitations on statutory safeguards is the insistence that, to qualify for most rights, you must have built up a specified period of continuous employment. If that period has been broken, or if you work only part-time, the small print of the legislation might exclude you from its scope.

The qualifying period for the right to statutory redundancy pay is two years. The same is generally true of unfair dismissal rights, although if the reason for dismissal was trade union-related, there is no qualifying period at all. You must have worked for 13 weeks to be entitled to a statutory statement of the main terms of your employment. But you may be able to complain to a tribunal that you have been discriminated against on the grounds of sex or race, even if the company concerned never offered you a job.

The age limit in unfair dismissal law was discussed in Chapter 6; that applicable to redundancy payment rights was mentioned in Chapter 17. Many other rights are not subject to any age limit at all.

Again, it is a peculiarity of unfair dismissal law that an industrial tribunal does not have the power to consider the fairness of dismissal where at the time of dismissal the employer was conducting a lockout or the employee was taking part in a strike or other industrial action. This was one of the trump cards of News International in its dispute with the print workers in 1986–87. On the other hand, an employer who dismisses a redundant employee for going on strike during his notice period will still have to make him a redundancy payment unless he serves a 'notice of extension' in accordance with the Consolidation Act requiring him to make up the time lost through the strike.

Much may hinge upon points that the typical executive might understandably regard as irritating technicalities. Clearly, before you make too many assumptions about the strength of your position in law, it is vital to check the precise rules that apply to you.

Nor is that all. Most statutory rights have to be enforced within a strict time limit. A tribunal cannot consider an unfair dismissal complaint unless it is presented during a three-month period beginning with the effective date of termination. In a rare case where it was not reasonably practicable for the complaint to be presented within that time span, that complaint must be made within such further period as the tribunal considers reasonable.

You will not be entitled to state redundancy pay, on the other hand, unless within six months from the dismissal date:

(a) the payment has been agreed and paid; or
(b) you have claimed the payment by written notice to your employer; or
(c) you have made a complaint to an industrial tribunal; or
(d) you have lodged an unfair dismissal claim.

The time limit can be extended by a further six months if it appears to be 'just and equitable' to do so.

It has already been mentioned that, in contrast, there is generally a six-year limitation period for instituting proceedings in respect of breach of contract in the civil courts.

In all cases, you would be wise to avoid waiting until the last minute. As any solicitor will tell you, time limits can be missed all too easily. Most of the rules are applied strictly and it is hard to imagine any outcome more frustrating than for your legitimate claim to fail simply because you have been guilty of delay. To secure your rights, be prepared to respond rapidly when problems occur.

Chapter 21

Moving Elsewhere

21.1 References

No employee can insist upon being given a reference when he leaves a job, unless (as hardly ever happens) his contract specifically entitles him to one. Not every employer is willing to give an open 'to whom it may concern' reference. Some are even reluctant to respond positively when approached directly by another prospective employer. But, if a reference is given, it ought to be accurate.

In the (one hopes, very unlikely) event that you are defamed by a reference, the normal rules of libel and slander apply. You may also be able to sue for damages if your employer, past or present, fails to take care to ensure that his comments are based on correct information.

This point emerged in a 1986 case in which the High Court accepted that a person seeking a job relies on the accuracy of a reference about his character and capabilities even if he does not actually ask for it himself. So if you lose the chance of a job because of a mistakenly critical reference, it is worth considering whether there is anything to be gained from taking legal action.

21.2 Written statement of reasons for dismissal

You are entitled to a written statement of the reasons for your dismissal if you have been employed for two years or more.

This is a modern statutory right. The thinking behind it, according to the Employment Appeal Tribunal, is to enable you to have a 'piece of paper' explaining why you were dismissed to show to prospective employers. In this respect, obtaining a written statement is very much second best to persuading your ex-employer to provide a suitably positive reference.

Asking for a written statement is often a prelude to presenting an unfair dismissal claim. If, for example, the reasons described seem unfair or conflict with what was said to you at the time of your dismissal, and you are eligible for unfair dismissal rights, the next step might be for you to make a complaint to the industrial tribunal.

Your request for a statement of reasons may be either verbal or written. It is better to put it in writing, and keep a copy, so that you have proof of when the request was made. You are entitled to a response within 14 days.

If your former employer unreasonably refuses to supply a statement, or if the information that he gives is inadequate or untrue, you may apply to a tribunal which:

1. may declare what the real reasons for your dismissal were; and
2. should award you two weeks' pay.

A mere failure to respond, within the 14-day time limit or at all, does not necessarily amount to an unreasonable refusal. The tribunal will look at the explanation for the employer's behaviour before reaching a decision.

The tribunal will also have considerable discretion in deciding whether or not the reasons given are adequate. Clearly, the statement should contain a sensible account of why you lost your job, but a lengthy screed will seldom be called for. You should not expect to receive a detailed résumé of your employment history with the company.

21.3 How free are you to move?

As we saw in Chapter 5, your freedom to move elsewhere may be limited in a number of ways. This is so even if your contract contains no specific restrictive covenants.

A case involving the intensely competitive newspaper industry demonstrates what may happen. *Evening Standard Co Ltd v Henderson* (1987) concerned a production manager whose contract said that while he was employed, 'on no account are you to engage in outside work'. He told his company that he proposed to join a rival newspaper, giving two months' notice, rather than the 12 months' notice required by his contract.

His employers offered to pay him in full until the 12-month period expired and the High Court granted them an injunction, preventing Mr Henderson from leaving prematurely. He could not argue that, if he was not allowed to start his new job, he would starve.

Even after your job has clearly come to an end, you need to beware of breaking obligations that remain legally binding upon you, such as the duty not to disclose trade secrets. Naturally, you will have more room for manoeuvre if you have avoided agreeing to detailed and specific restraints.

An interesting illustration of the way in which the legal principles discussed earlier actually operate occurred in *Faccenda Chicken Ltd v Fowler* (1986). This case concerned a man who set up in competition with the business that had previously employed him. He advertised for staff, and eight former colleagues joined him. They were not subject to service contracts containing restrictive covenants. Soon they were selling goods to Faccenda's customers at lower prices, operating along the same routes as Faccenda and generally making calls earlier in the week than Faccenda.

Faccenda argued that its former employees had made improper use of a 'package' of confidential information, ie names and addresses of customers, the best routes to take to reach them, details of their usual requirements, times of Faccenda's usual deliveries and, above all, information about Faccenda's prices.

The Court of Appeal considered that the information did not amount to a trade secret. It had to be known by employees to do their jobs and was widely known by relatively junior members of staff. It could be memorised easily and no warning had been given about its sensitivity. Accordingly, Faccenda's claim failed.

Study any written restrictions in your agreement with particular care. To what extent do they appear to preclude you from making use of the skills and knowledge that you have acquired and competing with the people for whom you used to work? If you overstep the mark, you may find yourself involved in a costly legal fight, with your former employers seeking an injunction or damages or both for breach of contract. Take advice urgently if your intended course of action seems to be at all risky.

21.4 Aggressive recruiting

You may want to invite former colleagues to work for or with you in your new sphere. If so, find out what their notice obligations are.

You should aim to avoid inducing them to break their contracts by walking out without either giving that notice or agreeing that the notice period be shortened. Remember what was said in Chapter 1, section 1.7, on this point. Your business plans could be severely jeopardised if you become embroiled in litigation started by the company that you used to work for.

21.5 Taking stock

We live in an age of increasing employee mobility. When the time comes for you to move on, whether or not you leave through your own choice, it is worth taking stock for a moment.

However many difficulties you have faced, what is certain is that you will have kept on learning, both about the realities of the business world and about yourself. No one ever knows it all, but the experience should prove invaluable. In the end, if you keep your wits about you, there is every chance that not only will you get the best deal from your employer, you will also prove that you are worth it.

Appendices

1. Typical service agreement for a director or other senior executive

The sample agreement set out below illustrates many of the points made in the text. It is typical of standardised service agreements in that several of its key clauses are weighted in favour of the employer. It is not put forward here as a precedent of good drafting. As the text emphasises, it is desirable from the point of view of both employers and employees that an executive's contractual terms should be tailored to suit his individual circumstances.

THIS AGREEMENT is made on   One thousand nine hundred and   *BETWEEN   LIMITED* (registered in England No.   ) having its registered office at   (hereinafter called 'the Company') of the one part and   of   (hereinafter called 'the Employee') of the other part *WHEREBY IT IS AGREED* as follows:

1. Definitions
In this Agreement:

'Associated Company'	means a company which is from time to time a subsidiary or a holding company (as those expressions are defined by Section 736 of the Companies Act 1985) of the Company or a subsidiary (other than the Company) of a holding company of the Company
'the Board'	means the Board of Directors from time to time of the Company
'the Business of the Company'	means the business of

2. Term of Employment
The Employee shall serve the Company as   Director or in such other capacity of an equivalent status as the Company may reasonably require from the date hereof unless and until his employment hereunder shall be determined in accordance with clause 9 hereof or by either party giving to the other not less than   months' notice in writing

3. Duties etc
During the continuance of his employment hereunder the Employee shall:

(a) exercise such powers and perform such duties (being duties appropriate to his status, qualifications and experience) in relation to the Business of the Company as may from time to time be vested in or assigned to him by the Board and shall comply with all reasonable directions from time to time given to him by the Board and with all rules and regulations from time to time laid down by the Company concerning its employees *PROVIDED THAT* the Employee's normal place of work (excluding business travelling) shall be at

(b) during the normal working hours specified in the Schedule hereto (unless prevented by ill health or accident and except during holidays permitted by this Agreement) devote the whole of his time attention and abilities to carrying out his duties hereunder

(c) carry out his duties in a proper loyal and efficient manner and shall use his best endeavours to promote the interests and reputation of the Company and its Associated Companies and not do anything which is to their detriment

(d) travel to such places (whether within or outside the United Kingdom) and in such manner and on such occasions as the Company may from time to time reasonably require

(e) not without the prior written consent of the Company undertake any other business or profession or be or become an employee or agent of any other company firm or person or assist or have any financial interest in any other business or profession *PROVIDED THAT* nothing in this paragraph shall preclude the Employee from holding or acquiring less than 5 per cent of the issued shares or other securities of any other company which are quoted on any recognised Stock Exchange by way of *bona fide* investment only unless the Company shall require him to do so in any particular case on the ground that such other company is or may be carrying on a business competing or tending to compete with the Business of the Company

4. Inventions etc

(a) It shall be part of the normal duties of the Employee at all times to consider in what manner and by what new methods or devices the products, services, processes, equipment or systems of the Company, or any Associated Company, with which he is concerned or for which he is responsible might be improved, and promptly to give to the Secretary of the Company full details of any invention or improvement which he may from time to time make or discover in the course of his duties, and to further the interests of the Company with regard thereto. Subject to any contrary provisions of the Patents Act 1977 where applicable, the Company shall be entitled free of charge to the sole ownership of any such invention or improvement and, so far as the law permits, to the exclusive use thereof

(b) The Employee shall, if and whenever required so to do by the Company, at the expense of the Company apply or join with the Company in applying for letters patent or other protection in any part of the world for any such discovery invention or process as aforesaid and shall at the expense of the Company execute and do or procure to be executed or done all instruments and things necessary for vesting the said letters patent or other protection when obtained and all right title and interest to and in the same in the Company or in such other person as the Company may require and the Company shall (and shall procure that any such other person shall) hold the same and all such right title and interest to and in the same upon trust for itself and (to the extent that he is entitled thereto by Section 39 of the Patents Act 1977) the Employee according to its and his respective interests therein

(c) Any document drawing design or program or other literary or artistic work made or created by the Employee during the continuance of his period of employment hereunder which concerns or relates to the Business of the Company and the copyright therein shall (whether or not the work was made at the direction of the Company or was intended to benefit the Company) belong to the Company and to the extent that such copyright is not otherwise vested in the Company the Employee *HEREBY ASSIGNS* the same to the Company

(d) For the purpose of this clause the Employee *HEREBY IRREVOCABLY AUTHORISES* the Company as his attorney in his name to execute and do any documents or things which are required in order to give effect to the provisions of this clause and the Company is hereby empowered to appoint and remove at pleasure any person as agent and substitute for and on behalf of the Company in respect of all or any of the matters aforesaid

5. **Confidential Information**
   (a) The Employee shall during the continuance of his period of employment hereunder and after the termination thereof (howsoever occasioned) observe strict secrecy as to the affairs dealings and concerns of the Company and shall not either during the continuance of his employment hereunder or at any time thereafter except in the proper course of his duties hereunder or with the prior written consent of the Board divulge or communicate to any third party except to another employee of the Company authorised to receive the same or turn to his own account and shall use his best endeavours to prevent the publication or disclosure of any trade secret or other confidential information concerning the organisation business or finances of the Company or any of its dealings transactions affairs customers or clients which are within or may come to his knowledge during the course of his engagement and shall not use or attempt to use any knowledge or information which he may acquire as aforesaid in any manner which may injure or cause loss whether directly or indirectly to the Company or use his personal knowledge of or influence over any customers clients suppliers or contractors of the Company so as to take advantage of the Company's trade or business connections or utilise information confidentially obtained by him *PROVIDED THAT* the provisions of this clause shall cease to apply to information which enters the public domain other than directly or indirectly by reason of the default of the Employee
   (b) the provisions of sub-clause (a) of this clause shall apply *mutatis mutandis* in relation to each Associated Company

6. **Remuneration**
   (a) The Employee shall be paid by way of remuneration for his services during his employment hereunder a salary at the rate of £   per annum. Such salary shall be paid by equal monthly instalments in arrears on the last day of every month and shall accrue from day to day. Such salary shall be reviewed on the   of each year and shall be increased provided that the performance of the Employee in the opinion of the Board justified such increase. Notwithstanding anything to the contrary contained in the Articles of Association of the Company or of any Associated Company the Employee shall not be entitled to any other remuneration either as director or

employee of the Company or any Associated Company and the Employee shall as the Company may direct either effectually waive his right to any such remuneration on account for and pay over the same to the Company forthwith upon receipt

(b) In case the Employee shall at any time be prevented by illness or accident or other incapacity from properly performing his duties hereunder and shall if required furnish the Company with evidence of such incapacity he shall (subject as hereinafter provided) be entitled to receive:

> (i) his full remuneration for the first consecutive period of three months and
>
> (ii) one-half of his remuneration for any further consecutive period not exceeding three months in aggregate

during which such incapacity shall continue and thereafter the Employee shall receive no other payment *PROVIDED THAT* there shall be deducted from any payments made by the Company pursuant to this clause the aggregate amount of any Social Security sickness or industrial injury benefits recoverable by or payable to the Employee

7. Expenses

The Company shall reimburse to the Employee all reasonable travel, accommodation, entertainment and other out-of-pocket expenses which he may from time to time properly incur in the exercise of his duties hereunder *PROVIDED THAT* the Company shall be entitled to require such expenses to be duly vouched by written evidence

8. Car

To assist him in the performance of his duties hereunder the Company shall during the continuance of his employment hereunder (subject to his being fully qualified to drive) provide for the Employee a motor car suitable for use by a person of his status and shall bear the cost of insuring testing taxing repairing and maintaining the same and shall reimburse the Employee all running expenses of the car properly incurred by him in connection with his duties hereunder. The Employee shall:

(a) take good care of the car and procure that the provisions and conditions of any policy of insurance relating thereto are observed;

(b) not permit such car to be taken out of the United Kingdom without the written consent of the Company; and

(c) return the car and its keys to the Company's registered office immediately upon the termination of his employment hereunder

9. Summary Termination

Without prejudice to any other right or remedy that the Company may have against the Employee the Company may determine the Employee's employment hereunder summarily by notice in writing if:

(a) a Receiving Order is made against him or he makes any arrangement or composition with his creditors or is convicted of an indictable offence (other than a motoring offence which does not result in the imposition of a sentence or imprisonment); or

(b) he becomes of unsound mind; or

(c) he is guilty of any gross misconduct, gross negligence or default or serious breach or non-observance of any of the stipulations herein contained; or

(d) he becomes incapacitated by illness or injury for a continuous period of six months; or

(e) he becomes prohibited by law from being a director of a company

10. Misrepresentation

The Employee shall not at any time make any untrue statement in relation to the Company or any Associated Company, and in particular shall not after the termination of his employment hereunder wrongfully represent himself as being employed by or connected with the Company or any Associated Company

11. Employee's Obligations Upon Termination

Upon the termination of his employment hereunder for any cause whatsoever the Employee shall:

(a) immediately deliver up to the Company all documents, statistics, accounts, records, programs and other items of whatsoever nature or description which may be in his possession or under his control which relate in any way to the business or affairs of the Company or of any Associated Company and no copies of any such documents as aforesaid or any part thereof shall be retained by him

(b) at any time thereafter forthwith upon the request of the Board resign without claim for compensation from any such office as a Director of the Company or of any Associated Company as he may hold at the time of such request and should he fail to do so the Company is *HEREBY IRREVOCABLY AUTHORISED* to appoint some person in his name and on his behalf to sign and do any documents or things which are required to give effect thereto

12. Restrictions After Termination

The Employee agrees that for a period of   after termination of his employment hereunder (howsoever caused) he shall not:

(a) either alone or jointly with others as employee, director or as agent for any person, firm, company or other organisation directly or indirectly carry on or be engaged or concerned in any business which competes with any aspect of the Business of the Company in which he shall have been personally concerned at the date of such termination and which is located less than   miles from an existing factory or office of the Company

(b) either on his own account or for any person directly or indirectly solicit interfere with or endeavour to entice from the Company any person who is then or was during the period of   preceding the date of such termination (a) a client (b) a customer (c) an employee of or (d) otherwise in the habit of dealing with the Company provided that such restrictions shall only apply to clients, customers, employees or other persons with whom the Employee shall have been personally concerned

and it is hereby agreed and declared that:

(i) each of the individual covenants on the part of the Employee contained in this clause shall be deemed to be a separate covenant and shall be so construed; and

(ii) the Company and the Employee consider the covenants contained herein to be reasonable in the circumstances pertaining to the Employee's employment but that in the event that any such restriction shall be found to be void but would be valid if some part thereof were deleted or the period or area of application reduced such restriction shall apply with such modification as may be necessary to render it valid and effective

13. Notices
Any notice in writing to be served hereunder may be given personally to the Employee or to the Secretary of the Company (as the case may be) or may be posted to the Company (for the attention of its Secretary) at its registered office for the time being or to the Employee either at his address given above or at his last known address. Any such notice sent by post shall be deemed served twenty-four hours after it is posted and in proving such service it shall be sufficient to prove that the notice was properly addressed and put in the post.

14. Headings
The headings to the clauses in the Agreement are included for convenience only and shall not affect the construction hereof

15. The Schedule
The provisions set out in the Schedule hereto as from time to time amended shall apply as if incorporated in this Agreement

16. Cancellation of Previous Agreements
As from the date hereof all previous agreements between the Company and the Employee relating to the employment of the Employee by the Company shall be deemed to have been cancelled

17. Governing Law
This Agreement shall be governed by and construed under English Law and each of the parties hereto submits to the jurisdiction of the English Courts as regards any claim or matter arising under this Agreement

IN WITNESS whereof this Agreement has been signed by or on behalf of the parties hereto the day and year first before written

SCHEDULE

(A) Normal Working Hours
Normal working hours are   am to   pm Monday to Friday inclusive with a lunch break from   to

(B) Work Outside Normal Hours
Where the Company considers necessary the Employee will be required to work outside or beyond normal working hours or at

weekends or on holidays and no extra payment will be made for such work

(C) Holidays
In addition to bank and other public holidays the Employee will be entitled to   weeks holiday in every calendar year to be taken at such time or times as may be approved by the Board. Unless and until his employment under this Agreement shall be determined under any provision thereof salary will continue to be payable during holidays. Holidays not taken in any calendar year or by the termination of his employment under this Agreement will be lost and upon termination of his employment the Employee will not be entitled to any accrued holiday pay or to any pay in lieu of holiday

(D) Pension
The Employee is a member of the Company's Retirement Benefit Scheme the rules of which (incorporating any changes from time to time made therein) are available for inspection at the Company Secretary's office at any time upon reasonable notice

(E) Continuous Employment
The Employee's employment with the Company which began on   counts as part of his continuous period of employment with the Company for the purpose of the Employment Protection (Consolidation) Act 1978

(F) Grievance and Disciplinary Procedure
In the event of the Employee wishing to seek redress of any grievance relating to his employment or if he is dissatisfied with any disciplinary decision relating to him he should first apply in person to the Managing Director. The Employee must then promptly answer (in writing if required) such questions (if any) as any member of the Board wishes to put to him on the matter before the Board comes to a decision. The decision of the Board on such matters shall be final

(G) Disciplinary Rules
Any disciplinary rules applicable to the Employee are specified in a file which is available for inspection at the Company Secretary's office at any time upon reasonable notice

SIGNED by   *SIGNED* by the Employee
on behalf of the Company   in the presence of:
in the presence of:

2. Table of cases and text section reference

Adams v G K N Sankey Ltd (1980) IRLR 416, 16.3, 19.3
Alexander v Standard Telephones & Cables Ltd (1990) IRLR 55, 20.3
BBC v Beckett (1983) IRLR 43, 2.5
Council of Engineering Institutions v Maddison (1976) IRLR 389, 19.5
Cowen v Haden Carrier Ltd (1982) IRLR 225, (1982) IRLR 314, 13.2
W E Cox Toner (International) Ltd v Crook (1981) IRLR 443, 15.4
Cresswell and others v Board of Inland Revenue (1984) IRLR 190, 8.4
Deeley v British Rail Engineering (1980) IRLR 147, 1.1
Dobie v Burns International Security Services (UK) Ltd (1984) IRLR 329, 9.2
East Lindsay District Council v Daubney (1977) IRLR 181, 11.3
Evening Standard Co Ltd v Henderson (1987) IRLR 64, 21.3
Faccenda Chicken Ltd v Fowler (1986) IRLR 69, 21.3
F C Gardner Ltd v Beresford (1978) IRLR 63, 15.2
Gill and others v Cape Contracts Ltd (1985) IRLR 499, 1.6
Goodman v Winchester and Alton Railway plc (1984) Industrial Relations Legal Information Bulletin 269, 20.2
Greer v Sketchley Ltd (1979) IRLR 445, 5.6
Hollister v National Farmers' Union (1979) IRLR 238, 8.5
International Computers Ltd v Kennedy (1981) IRLR 28, 13.3
International Sports Co Ltd v Thomson (1980) IRLR 340, 11.1
Janata Bank v Ahmed (1981) IRLR 457, 7.3, 10.4
Jones v Associated Tunnelling Co Ltd (1981) IRLR 477, 2.3
Litster v Forth Dry Dock & Engineering Co Ltd (1989) IRLR 161, 13.2
Littlewoods Organisation Ltd v Harris (1977) 1 All ER 1026, 5.6
Marley Tile Co Ltd v Johnson (1982) IRLR 75, 5.6
Marshall v Harland & Wolff Ltd (1972) IRLR 90, 11.1
Mears v Safecar Security Ltd (1982) IRLR 183, 2.5
Albert J Parsons & Sons Ltd v Parsons (1979) IRLR 117, 1.4
Payne v Spook Erection Ltd (1984) IRLR 219, 10.1, 12.1
Provident Financial Group plc and Whitegates Estate Agency Ltd v Hayward (1989) IRLR 84, 5.6
R S Components Ltd v Irwin (1974) 1 All ER 41, 8.5
Reiss Engineering Co Ltd v Harris (1985) IRLR 232, 5.3
Sayers v International Drilling Co NV (1971) 3 All ER 163, 7.3

Shove v Downs Surgical plc (1984) IRLR 17, 4.7, 18.3, 18.6, 18.7, 18.8
Stacey v Babcock Power Ltd (1986) IRLR 3, 14.6
Staffordshire County Council v Donovan (1981), 16.2
Stapp v Shaftesbury Society (1982) IRLR 326, 16.3
Strathclyde Regional Council v Porcelli (1986) IRLR 134, 9.3
Todd v British Midland Airways Ltd (1978) IRLR 370, 7.3
Wilson v Maynard Ship Building Consultants AB (1977) IRLR 491, 7.3
Wiltshire County Council v NATFHE and Guy (1980) IRLR 198, 16.2
Winterhalter Gastronom Ltd v Webb (1973) IRLR 120, 17.4
Young and Woods Ltd v West (1980) IRLR 201, 1.3

Useful Addresses

Advisory, Conciliation and Arbitration Service (ACAS)
Head Office
27 Wilton Street
London SW1X 7AZ
071-210 3000
Regional offices in Birmingham, Bristol, Cardiff, Fleet, Glasgow, Leeds, London, Manchester, Newcastle upon Tyne, Nottingham

Commission for Racial Equality
Elliot House
10–12 Allington Street
London SW1E 5EH
071-828 7022

Department of Employment
Head Office
Caxton House
Tothill Street
London SW1H 9NF
071-273 3000
Regional offices in Birmingham, Bristol, Cardiff, Edinburgh, Leeds, London, Manchester, Newcastle upon Tyne

Equal Opportunities Commission
Overseas House
Quay Street
Manchester M3 3HN
061-833 9244

Further Reading from Kogan Page

Career Counselling for Executives, Godfrey Golzen, 1988
Changing Your Job After 35: The Daily Telegraph Guide, 6th edition, Godfrey Golzen and Philip Plumbley, 1988
Job Sharing: A Practical Guide, Pam Walton, 1990
Living and Retiring Abroad: The Daily Telegraph Guide, 4th edition, Michael Furnell, 1990
Making the Most of Your Retirement, 2nd edition, Keith Hughes, 1989
Winning at Your Interview, Michael Stevens, 1989
Working Abroad: The Daily Telegraph Guide to Working and Living Overseas, 13th edition, 1990

Also by Martin Edwards

Dismissal Law: A Practical Guide for Management, 2nd edition, 1991

Index

Absence from work 86–91, 110
ACAS:
   Code of Practice 30–31, 93
   Conciliation officer 72, 157
   Discipline At Work handbook 83, 86, 93
Accommodation expenses 46, 68, 141
Advertisements 15–17, 70
Advisory, Conciliation and Arbitration Service, *see* ACAS
Agencies 16
Agreed procedures 108–9
Alternative employment 78, 85, 90, 106–7, 143
Ambiguity 123–4, 126–7
Appeals 95, 98–9, 128
Applications for jobs 16–17, 70
Appraisals, *see* Job appraisal
Arbitration 156–7
Associated employer 24, 37, 102
Attendance record 110

Base, *see* Place of work
Bonus 44, 140–41
Breach of contract, *see* Contract of employment

'Bumping' 102–3
Business transfer 35–6, 74, 82, 104

Car 44–5, 139–40, 171–2
Collective agreement 26
Commission 43, 140
Commission for Racial Equality 17, 72, 79
Company:
   director 16, 20, 62
   group 34, 37, 114, 150, 153
   handbook 30
   law 20, 62
   subsidiary 34, 37, 66–7, 167
Compensation:
   breach of contract 120, 121, 136–45
   discrimination 79
   for loss of office 149–50
   inducing breach of contract 23, 162–3
   inventions 50
   negligence 85
   unfair dismissal 129–35
   wrongful dismissal 120, 127, 136–45
Competition 48–57, 94, 161–3
Computer programs 38, 49, 169

Confidential information 16, 51-2, 94, 162, 170
Constructive dismissal 32, 38, 42, 62, 70, 74, 78, 115-22
Consultancy 152
Consultation 88-90, 104, 111-4
Continuous employment 24, 27, 30, 35-7, 60, 126-8, 158, 175
Contract of employment:
  generally 25-39
  breach of 66-7, 72, 94, 115-21, 127, 136-45, 153, 157
  existence of 18-20, 22
  illegal 24, 157
  implied terms 26, 29, 31-2, 39, 85, 116-17
  variation 28, 69, 72-4
  verbal 25
Contract of service, see Contract of employment
Contracting out 19, 61-2, 153-4
Contributory fault 139, 144
Copyright 38, 49-50, 169
Costs 131
COT3 (form) 154
COT4 (form) 154
Counter notice 126
County Court 137
Curriculum vitae 16, 70, 122
Customary arrangement 108-9
Customer pressure 77

Declaration 157
Defamation 160
Demotion 98, 115
Designs 49, 169
Directorship, see Company director
Disability 87, 110
Disciplinary proceedings 92-9, 116, 124, 175

record 110
rules 18, 27-8, 30-32
Discrimination
  race 17, 30, 78-9, 158
  sex 17, 30, 59, 78-9, 88, 158
Dishonesty 94-96
Disloyalty, see Competition
Dismissal date 126-8
Disobedience 93-4
Driving disqualification 95-6
Drunkenness 94

Early retirement, see Retirement
Economic duress 154
Effective date of termination, see Dismissal date
Employment agencies, see Agencies
Equal Opportunities Commission 17, 72, 79
Equal pay 26
Equality clause 26
Exchange rate 67
Ex-gratia payments 135
Expatriates, see Overseas work
Expenses 39, 44, 68, 131, 134, 171

Fixed-term contracts 28, 61-2, 103, 125
Flexibility provisions 108-9, 115
Freedom to recruit 17
Fringe benefits 40-47, 106, 133-4, 138-41
Frustration of contract 67, 86-7, 122

Garden leave 53-5, 117
Gifts 149
Golden handcuff 41-2

Golden handshake 142, 149–50
Golden hello 41
Golden parachute 41–2
Governing law 63–4, 174
Government Actuary's
 Department 134, 140
Grievance procedure 28, 71,
 118, 175
Gross misconduct, *see*
 Misconduct
Gross negligence 83–4
Group of companies, *see*
 Company
Guarantee by parent company
 66–7

High Court 136, 145, 147
High-risk jobs 84
Holiday pay 28, 44, 175
Holidays 28, 135, 175
Hours of work 28, 106–7, 174–5
Hurt feelings 132, 141–2

Illegality, *see* Contract of
 employment
Ill-health, *see* Sickness
Implied terms, *see* Contract of
 employment
Incompetence 80–85, 131
Inconsistency 82, 95
Indemnity 67
Index-linking 43
Industrial action 158
Industrial tribunal:
 breach of contract claims
  136–7
 claim for failure to supply
  written reasons for
  dismissal 161
 discrimination claims 158
 redundancy payment claims
  159

unfair dismissal claims 118,
 129–35, 158–9
Wages Act claims 157
Injunction 157
Intransigence 84
Inventions 38, 50–51, 168–9

Job:
 application 16, 70, 143
 appraisal 70, 80–81
 description 38, 70, 80
 file 16, 70, 82
 interview 16–17
 offer 17, 20–24, 26–7, 34,
  106–7
 performance 77, 80–85, 110
 plan 80
 satisfaction 117
 title 28, 37–8

Know-how 51

Language tuition 68
Lay-off 101
Legal expenses insurance 71
Legal representation 97
Length of service 77, 87, 90,
 109–10
Letter of appointment, *see* Job
 offer
Libel 160
Life insurance 46, 141
Loans 46
Lock-out 158
Loss of employment rights 134

Maternity leave 91
Meal allowance 46, 141
Medical opinion 89–90
Misconduct 92–9, 131
Misrepresentation 172
Mitigation of loss 134–5, 143

Mobility clause 38-9, 44, 101-2, 115-16
Mutual consent 124-5
Mutual trust and confidence 32, 115

Natural justice 92-3
Negligence, *see* Incompetence
Negotiation techniques 21, 23, 147-9
New technology 72-3, 106
Normal retiring age, *see* Retirement
Normal working hours, *see* Hours of work
Notice:
  generally 23, 27-8, 33, 58-62, 118, 125-8, 148
  reasonable 60-61
  statutory minimum 18, 60, 128, 138-9
Notice of extension 158

Outplacement counselling 46, 114, 152
Outside funding 103
Over-promotion 84-5
Overseas work, 33, 63-8
Overtime, *see* Hours of work

Part-time workers 27, 30, 36
Patents 50-51, 168-9
Paternity leave 46
Pay:
  generally 40-46, 67-8, 106-7, 110, 113, 170-71
  cut 114-15, 120
  deductions 137
  in lieu of notice 150-51
  increase 38, 42-3, 116-17
Pension scheme:
  generally 28, 45-6, 175
  contracting out 28
  valuation 134, 140
Personal circumstances 110
Personality clashes 76-9
Place of work 38-9, 64-6, 106, 115
Poaching, *see* Competition
Pregnancy 88
Private health care 46, 141
'Prescribed element' 133
Probationary period 24
Professional subscriptions 46, 141
Promotion 16, 84-5, 106
Proper law, *see* Governing law
Protective award 111

Recoupment notice 133
Recruitment, *see* Freedom to recruit
Reduction in work 101-3
Redundancy:
  automatically unfair 108
  consultation 111-14
  definition 100-107
  payments 36, 46, 61, 100-101, 130-31, 148, 158-9
  rebate 101
  selection 108-11
  volunteers 105
Re-engagement 129
References 21, 151, 160
Reinstatement 129
Relocation, *see* Expenses *and* Mobility clause
Reorganisation 73-4, 103, 120
Repatriation 67
Reputation 117
Resignation 123-6, 173
Restrictive covenants 48-57, 73, 148, 161-2, 173
Retail Prices Index 43

Retirement 59, 106
Re-training 46, 151–2
Right to work 117
Rolling contract 62

Sabbaticals 46
Salary, *see* Pay
Secondment 35
Self-employment 18–20
Service agreement, *see* Contract of employment
Settlement, *see* Termination package
Sexual harassment 78, 116
Share incentive schemes 45, 141, 151
Shareholdings 53, 151, 168
Short-term contracts 36
Short time 101
Sickness:
   generally 28, 36, 86–91, 94, 139
   benefits 133
   pay 18–19, 28, 31–2, 44, 86, 171
Slander 160
Social security benefits 133
Status 106, 120
Statutory statement 27–30
Strike 158
Sub-contracting work 103
Subsidiary company, *see* Company
Suspected misconduct 96
Suspension 98, 119

Tape recorded conversations 70–71
Targets 81–2
Tax considerations 18–20, 24, 40–45, 67–8, 142–3, 149–51

Telephone expenses, 46, 141
Temporary cessation of work 36–7
Termination package 130, 142–3, 146–54
Theft, *see* Dishonesty
Time limits:
   generally 126–7, 137–8
   redundancy payment claims 158–9
   unfair dismissal claims 158–9
Top-slicing 150
Trade secrets 51–2, 162
Trade union 26, 108–9, 111–12
Trade union activities 27, 158
Training and support 82
Transfer of business, *see* Business transfer
Trial period 107
Tribunals, *see* Industrial Tribunal

Ultimatums, 37, 124
Unemployment benefit 143
Unfair dismissal:
   compared with wrongful dismissal claim 144–5
   entitlement to claim 19–20, 24, 59, 61–2, 74
   principles 80–85, 93, 96–7, 108–14, 120–21, 144–5, 148

Violence 94

Wages Act 137
Warnings 97–8
'Week's pay' 130, 161
Witness 93, 97
Words of dismissal 123–5

186 Index

Words of resignation, *see* Ambiguity *and* Resignation
Written particulars, *see* Statutory statement
Written reasons for dismissal 160–61
Wrongful dismissal, *see* Breach of contract